Value added tax

Value added tax

Alan A Tait, MA, PhD

Professor of Financial and Monetary Economics,
The University of Strathclyde

London · New York · St Louis · San Francisco · Düsseldorf
Johannesburg · Kuala Lumpur · Mexico · Montreal · New Delhi
Panama · Rio de Janeiro · Singapore · Sydney · Toronto

Published by

McGRAW-HILL Book Company (UK) Limited
MAIDENHEAD . BERKSHIRE . ENGLAND

---

07 094238 2

PRINTED AND BOUND IN GREAT BRITAIN
BY A. WHEATON & CO., EXETER

Contents

v

Preface

The value added tax is important because it has been adopted, for better or for worse, as the major sales tax of the European Economic Community. Any country joining the Community as a full member is obliged to replace its existing sales taxes by the VAT. (It is perhaps indicative of British attitudes towards things European, that the British prefer to change the European initials TVA to a variation of their own, VAT, despite a simple interpretation of the widely accepted TVA—Tax on Value Added.)

The move from existing sales taxes to the VAT is a substantial policy change for most countries outside the EEC, and indeed for some of the countries within the Community, a change which some countries might not have undertaken had they remained outside the Community. It is clear, therefore, that the VAT is an important tax. Even if countries remain outside the EEC, it is certainly worth studying to see whether it might be advantageous to them to adopt the tax.

So whether countries do, or do not, join the EEC, the VAT is an interesting tax and one which is likely to affect the future tax policies of many countries. Countries need to assess the tax in detail for many reasons: they may be obliged to adopt it; they may want to adopt it; they might want to appreciate its weak points and improve on them; or they may want to reject it. What would happen if the VAT were introduced is impossible to predict accurately. The only way to know is to experiment, and yet experiments in economics are notoriously difficult to reverse.

That is why it is crucial to examine this tax in detail. It is hoped that this book will help to clarify some of the issues and potential difficulties, and suggest likely changes in prices, output, efficiency, and the balance of payments.

This book does not try to discuss the overall implications of tax harmonization in theory or in practice; this has been dealt with expertly by other writers.[1] A discussion of customs unions and tax harmonization would

[1] Shoup, C.S., Ed: *Fiscal Harmonisation in Common Markets*, Columbia University Press, New York, 1967.

Dosser, D: 'Theoretical Considerations for Tax Harmonisation', *Comparisons and Harmonisation of Public Revenue Systems*, International Institute of Public Finance, Brussels, 1966.

expand the content of this book and distract the reader from the main stream of thought which is concentrated on the actual forms of VAT used, their advantages and drawbacks, the changes possible in theory and in practice, and the desirable forms of VAT harmonization.

Chapter 1 makes some simple points about the VAT which set the scene for the rest of the book. The informed reader might skip this chapter; there is a summary at the end which outlines the main points.

Summaries are given at the end of chapters 4 to 8 inclusive. These are more technical chapters on the effects of different VAT substitutions and readers may prefer to look at the summaries to sort out their interests among the various points made in each chapter. The other chapters do not lend themselves to such treatment and the reader would be better advised to read the full text.

The number of arithmetical examples has been kept to a minimum. It is hoped the text which follows each example explains and summarizes the figures.

Any discussion of a specific tax balances uneasily between the desire to inform and comment on broad issues, and the temptation to poke into unsavoury alleys and byways. Some of the details were too tempting to be ignored, but it is hoped that even where enthusiasm for detail has triumphed the analysis informs and adds to the broader discussion.

There is already a body of literature on the VAT but much of it is scattered in journals and in documents published by the EEC or by the respective governments of the member countries. Overall, it is hoped that this book will provide an up-to-date, clear, comprehensive discussion of many of the practical and theoretical issues involved in the VAT.

Alan A. Tait

1. Calculating the value added tax

Some simple introductory points about the VAT

Some of the general objectives of the VAT are:

(a) To be a sales tax levied on the price at which a goods or services are transferred (sold) between businesses or persons.
(b) To be a general tax covering, as far as practicable, all goods and services.
(c) To use a simple proportional tax rate, or rates.
(d) To be levied on all stages of production and distribution including the retail stage.
(e) Not to discriminate between different forms of industrial organization.
(f) To represent precisely the same tax liability as a retail sales tax, unchanged by the number of transactions leading to the final retail sale.
(g) To be impartial between domestically produced goods and imported goods.
(h) To exempt exports.

The ways in which the VAT can achieve these objectives are discussed in the rest of this book. But it is worth while making one point at the start. All the effects noted above could be achieved by a retail sales tax. It could be general, cover all goods and services, tax the final product representing the contribution of all the previous stages of production and distribution, use a proportional tax rate, be non-discriminatory, impartial, and exempt exports. It would also be much more simple to administer. Why, then, is a retail sales tax not used?

The answer lies partly in the peculiar history of the development of VAT, and partly in some of the more far-fetched claims made for it. In this book, a retail sales tax will be the norm against which the VAT will be measured. To all intents and purposes, the retail sales tax is the main contender to the VAT, and is engagingly simple by comparison.

There is a second criteria to use in measuring the VAT. Some British commentators on the VAT write as though this tax was the panacea for all tax sicknesses. It is not. The Continental arguments in favour of the VAT system as opposed to the cascade sales tax system (see chapter 2) are straightforward. In Britain and the EFTA countries, the VAT might replace purchase taxes, turnover and wholesale taxes, and perhaps could be used to reduce direct taxes on businesses and individuals, and to increase transfer payments. This makes the issues much more complex. No one could claim with rigorous objectivity that the advantages or disadvantages of the VAT are clear cut.

The first need is to explain how the tax liability is calculated. In doing this, the form of the tax is explained, and the various optional ways of levying VAT are made clear.

Calculating the value added

There are many descriptions of the VAT[1]. Some are confusing; the terminology of one sometimes appears to contradict another, definitions are not made plain, and texts are sometimes turgid. Perhaps this is in the nature of the beast, but the relationships will be outlined again, in what is hoped is a clear format. Once the eight types of VAT are understood, many of the examples and discussions which follow will be easier to appreciate.

A tax on value added is, briefly, a tax levied on businesses on the value they add to their purchases of raw materials and goods and services. Leaving aside the problem of capital and stocks, we can represent this by writing value added (V/A), equals total output (O), minus total input (I) of purchases on current account.

$$V/A = O - I \qquad\qquad (a)$$

Clearly, the difference between output and the inputs of raw materials, energy, containers, etc., is the payments of wages and salaries (W), and the residual, which we will call profit (P).

$$O - I = W + P \qquad\qquad (b)$$

From (a) $\qquad\qquad V/A = O - I = W + P \qquad\qquad (c)$

So value added can be derived either by *subtraction* (O − I) or by *addition* (W + P). These forms of calculation are sometimes called the subtractive (or subtraction) method and the additive method (or procedure or process).[2]

[1] See especially: Sullivan, C. K: *The Tax on Value Added*, Columbia University Press, New York, 1965, Chapter 1.

Schmölder, G: *Turnover Taxes*, International Bureau of Fiscal Documentation, Amsterdam, 1966, p. 58 et seq.

Committee on Turnover Taxation, *Report*, Cmnd. 2300, HMSO, London, March 1964. (The Richardson Committee), Chapters 2 and 7.

[2] See Sullivan C. K., op. cit., p. 7–11.

Schmölder G., op. cit., p. 58–59.

The tax rate (t) on value added (tV/A) can then be applied in at least four ways.

From (c)

$$tV/A = t (W + P) \qquad (d)$$
$$tV/A = tW + tP \qquad (e)$$
$$tV/A = t (O - I) \qquad (f)$$
$$t/VA = tO - tI \qquad (g)$$

Though (e) and (g) appear mathematically identical to (d) and (f) respectively, in actual administration they are not, as will be shown later.

A simple numerical example should make clear the distinction between the addition and subtraction calculations.

Table 1.1

Distinction between addition and subtraction calculations

	Price exclusive of tax £	Tax rate %	Tax paid £	Price inclusive of tax £
Inputs: Raw materials	100	20	20	120
Energy	100	20	20	120
	200		40	240
Value added: Wages and profits	100	20	20	120
Output	300	20	60	360

Tax liability by addition from (d) : t (W + P) = 0.2 (100) = 20
Tax liability by subtraction from (f) : t (O − I) = 0.2 (300–200) = 20

Price exclusive or inclusive of tax. The example above is based on the tax rate levied on a price *excluding* the VAT element. This is the form recommended by the EEC for calculating the tax on value added and has been adopted by Germany and Denmark, On the other hand, France has used, and continues to use, a tax based on a price including the tax element. This distinction can be shown by repeating the example above ensuring that the price *exclusive* of tax (the first column) is kept the same as that in Table 1.1.

If method (f) is used, t (O − I), then the tax rate employed is not the nominal one of 20%, as 20% of O − I = 100 would only be £20. Instead, an *effective* rate of 25% is used on the *tax inclusive* price to yield £25, leaving the price exclusive of tax the same as it was before, £100. Because of the confusion between nominal and effective rates (and for other reasons which will be shown later), the more usual method of calculation is by formula (g), tO — tI, as follows.

The nominal rate (20%) is applied to the final price of the output £375 (tO) yielding £75. The nominal rate is also applied to the invoice price (tax inclusive) of the inputs £250 (tI) to yield £50. The tax on inputs is set against the tax on output, £75 — £50, leaving £25 as the tax liability on the firm's value added.

Table 1.2

Distinction between inclusive and exclusive prices

	Price exclusive of tax £	Tax rate %	Tax paid £	Price inclusive of tax £
Inputs:				
Raw materials	100	20	25	125
Energy	100	20	25	125
	200		50	250
Value added:				
Wages and profits	100		25	125
Output	300	20	75	375

By this *subtractive* method the firm's value added is computed only 'indirectly' through the taxes on inputs and the taxes on output. This is contrasted with the method (f) described above, where the tax rate is applied 'directly' to the value added. Thus (f) is sometimes known as the 'direct subtractive method', and (g) as the 'indirect subtractive method'.

This distinction between 'direct' and 'indirect' methods is also applied to (d) and (e) respectively. The direct method is sometimes called the 'accounts method' and the indirect the 'invoice method'.

A further complication arises when the direct subtractive method is called the 'prior turnover deduction' method, or sometimes even the 'cost subtraction method', and the indirect subtractive method is known as the 'prior tax deduction' method.[3] For the rest of this book the terms additive and subtractive, and direct and indirect will be used. (See Table 1.3.)

Both direct and indirect methods when applied to prices *inclusive* of tax involve an effective rate of tax higher than the nominal rate. Thus, in France, a rate of 20% is actually a rate of 25%. (For a complete discussion of this point see chapter 5.)

[3] Schmölder G., op. cit.
Missorten, W.: 'Some Problems in Implementing a Tax on Value Added', *National Tax Journal*, December 1968.

Summary:

(a) Value added can be calculated by either addition or subtraction.
(b) The tax rate can be levied on either a tax exclusive base, or a tax inclusive base. If the rate is levied on a tax inclusive base, then a distinction must be made between the nominal and effective rates. The effective rate will always be higher.
(c) On either a tax exclusive or tax inclusive base, there are two methods of calculating the tax, the direct and the indirect. This makes eight basic choices for tax calculation.

Table 1.3
Summary of the eight forms of VAT

	By addition		By subtraction	
	Tax exclusive	Tax inclusive	Tax exclusive	Tax inclusive
Direct	$t_n(W + P)$	$t_e(W + P)$	$t_n(O - I)$	$t_e(O - I)$
Indirect	$t_nW + t_nP$	$t_eW + t_eP$	$\boxed{t_nO - t_nI}$ *	$t_eO - t_eI$

Where t_n = nominal tax rate $\qquad$ t_e = effective tax rate
$\qquad$ W = wages and salaries $\qquad$ P = profits
$\qquad$ O = output (sales) on current account $\quad$ I = inputs (purchases) on current account
$\quad$ * This square represents the choice of the EEC.

2. The EEC choice of value added tax

A little history

The value added tax did not spring fully formed from the head of the Neumark Commission.[1] It evolved through successive attempts to reduce the inequities of the cascade turnover tax which was the sales tax commonly used by the countries now forming the EEC.

Table 2.1 is a summary of the evolution of the French VAT side by side with the development of the German sales taxes and the British purchase tax.

Both France and Germany had general taxes on firms' turnovers (transactions) in the early 'twenties. At low rates, e.g., 0·5% in Germany, they taxed each sale with no offset for previous tax payments. By this method, a cascade element is introduced as the tax is levied on a price which already includes tax (the tax on tax cascade), and second, where a standard mark-up may be maintained on a price including tax (the mark-up cascade). The disadvantages of this sort of taxation are well known;[2] briefly, it encourages vertical integration because each inter-firm sale which can be eliminated reduces total tax liability; it penalizes specialization for the same reason; and it is impossible to know exactly the tax content of a price at any particular stage of production, which makes sales tax adjustments at country borders arbitrary.

The French tackled the problem of the unsatisfactory cascade by substituting for the old transaction tax, taxes on the sale of particular goods at a single stage of production. For a time, 1926 to 1936, the cascade tax and the single-stage purchase tax ran together. By 1936, the old cascade transaction tax was clearly undesirable, and it and the newer single-stage purchase tax were both replaced by a new single-stage production tax.

This tax was levied on a wide range of goods, including many used as raw materials and components for further manufacture. To avoid reintro-

---

[1] *Report of the Fiscal and Financial Committee of the EEC*, 'The Neumark Report', Brussels 1958.

[2] Richardson Committee, op. cit., chapter 2.

Table 2.1
The evolution of the VAT

Year	France	Germany	Britain
1918		Cascade tax of 0·5%	
1920	Cascade transactions tax		
1926	Single-stage purchase taxes (*taxes uniques*)		
1936	Transactions tax and *taxes unique* abolished and start of the 'suspension of tax' with a productions tax		
1940			Purchase tax introduced
1943			PT upper rate at 100%
1947			PT upper rate at 125%
1948	'Suspension of tax' replaced by 'fractional payments' and the 'physical deduction'		
1951		Cascade tax reaches 4%	
1954	'Financial deduction' introduced to exempt most capital purchases. The name VAT created		
1955			New low rate for clothing and furniture.
1958			Number of rates reduced and 'spread' compressed
1962			Low rates consolidated into a 10% rate and top rates reduced to 45%
1963			Only three rates operated, 10%, 15% and 25%
1968	Extension of VAT to wholesale and retail trade	Introduction of the EEC model VAT	Expanded to four rates with 'luxury' rate of 50%
1970	All members of EEC to adopt VAT*		

* Belgium and Italy failed to comply with this time limit.

ducing cascades, the famous *regime suspensif* was introduced. This exempted a producer from paying tax on goods which were physically consumed in his production process. Unfortunately, the suspension of tax did not operate for capital goods and they were still taxed (discriminated against), and this impeded the modernization of industry and, because such a tax could not be remitted on exported goods, restricted exports.

The big change came in 1948 when, instead of the suspension of tax, the system of fractional payments was introduced. It is this fractional payment which forms the unique contribution of the VAT. Instead of transferring the goods between producers tax free, i.e., with tax suspended, purchasers were allowed to offset the amount of tax already paid on the good against their own tax liability. In this way, purchasers only paid tax on the value they added to the inputs they bought. This is the origin of the indirect method of assessing tax liability described in chapter 1.

This fractional payment still taxed capital goods. The final step in the evolution of the VAT allowed the tax content of capital goods to be offset against total tax liability. This was known as the 'financial deduction' to distinguish it from the 1948 'physical deduction'. The two deductions, one for the tax content of raw materials, and the other for the tax content of capital goods, are together known as the 'credit offset' under the EEC version of the VAT. This was the moment when Monsieur Lauré coined the name *Taxe sur la Valeur Ajoutée*—the TVA (or VAT as it is known in Britain).

During the 'fifties the Germans met the same problems with the cascade taxes which the French had met earlier. The incentive to turn the successive stages of production into a single taxable unit (thereby eliminating the cascade elements of sales between separate firms) was met by some rough and ready justice when vertically integrated firms in textiles were taxed at higher rates than firms which specialized. Likewise, wholesalers who carried out no processing were taxed at a special low rate.

Clearly, such approximate adjustments could not cope with the numerous associations thrown up by modern industry. Even more striking was the inequity of border tax adjustments. As the cascade tax content of a German export could not be calculated accurately, the rebates for taxes on goods exported had to be estimated (and of course, could not be equal to the actual tax content which could be different between two identical goods depending on the number of stages of production, the costs of inputs, and the profit margins). 'The result was a very lengthy list of export commodities and their respective rates of restitution.'[3] Similarly, to make sure the tax content of imports was equal to that of domestically produced goods, some cavalier treatment of goods on an average basis was used.

The scope such approximation gave for hidden protection for domestic production (by deliberately overestimating the tax content of imports)

[3] Rybczynski T. M., Ed: *The Value Added Tax: The U.K. Position and the European Experience*, Blackwell, Oxford, 1969, p. 31.

and subsidies to exporters (by overestimating the tax content of exports) engendered suspicion abroad and led to international criticism. The higher the rates of cascade tax, the greater are the incentives to integration and the larger the opportunities for concealed protection. Dissatisfaction was such that the Germans engineered the introduction of the VAT in 1968, two years earlier than the EEC required.

So the VAT is a product of successive adjustments by Governments on the Continent, and was particularly suited to countries transforming their sales taxes from a cascade tax. Whether it is equally suitable for countries with single-stage wholesale and retail sales taxes, or for replacing, in part, or wholly, some company and personal income taxes, is another matter entirely.

The additive and subtractive methods compared

Though the EEC has chosen the subtractive, tax exclusive, indirect method of calculating tax liability under the VAT system, and though this discussion is within the context of that system, it is worth while outlining the background to this choice for two reasons. First, it emphasizes the other options and isolates some of the peculiarities of the EEC choice, and second, it leads on to the choice of rates.

The basic decision is whether to assess value added by addition or subtraction. Five main arguments can be isolated, three in favour of using the addition computation, and two against.

(a) The main advantage of the additive method is simplicity. The concepts of profit and of wages are already used by businessmen and conform with conventional accountancy. (This is why Japanese accountants when considering a VAT for Japan favoured the additive method.)[4] Value added, as a difference between inputs and outputs, is not so simple in theory, and in practice becomes much less simple. It is worth pointing out that when more than one rate is used, the close relationship between the accounting and additive methods is substantially weakened.

(b) A second advantage is that the additive method identifies the components of value added. It makes explicit what, at first, is taxed, i.e., profits and wages. Of course, if the *intention* is to create a tax on consumption by ensuring that the VAT is passed forward fully, then this identification of the tax with wages and profits is needless. Indeed, it could be misleading. To emphasize the consumption tax nature of the EEC VAT, the Commission deliberately looked towards the subtractive method rather than the additive. But it is worth noting that many of the persuasive arguments in favour of VAT in promoting business efficiency are based on the assumption that the VAT is *not* passed forward.

[4] Sullivan C. K: *The Tax on Value Added*, Columbia University Press, New York, 1965, p. 138.

(c) Another advantage of the additive method is that it lessens the inflationary impact of a tax substitution. The main criticism by the Richardson Report was that the substitution of a VAT for a profits tax would be inflationary. This was because businessmen viewed the exchange as a substitution of profits taxation, which would not be reflected in lower prices, by a sales tax which would result in higher prices. This criticism is diluted if the additive method is considered. With the additive method, the change could well be viewed as a switch from one form of profits taxation to another. Of course, the whole argument is highly subjective as it depends on the reaction of businessmen to profits taxation and sales taxation (see chapter 7). However, two taxes on profits (value added by addition and corporate profits taxes) are more likely to be thought interchangeable, than a corporate profits tax and a sales tax, i.e., value added by subtraction, so the conclusions of the Richardson Report that prices would rise do not hold. This is important when it is remembered that on this basic supposition it was held that the substitution would mean price increases which would reduce international competitiveness and worsen the balance of payments on current account, etc. This was a cornerstone of the rejection of VAT by the Royal Commission. Our argument here is that a substitution of VAT by addition would not be so likely to increase prices as a substitution by subtraction.

(d) A tax on the aggregate of wages and profits, $[t (W + P)]$, has one outstanding disadvantage, it is only sensible on an annual basis. Most firms draw up their Profit and Loss Account once a year and, therefore, only know their profits after the end of the trading year. This would turn the VAT into an annual tax, instead of a monthly tax, which would reduce the revenue flow and lessen the statistical information derived from the VAT returns (see chapter 9). It is fair to point out that if the indirect method of assessing value added by addition were adopted, $(tW + tP)$, then the annual character need only apply to that part of the tax on profits (tP); the tax on wages (tW) could be collected weekly or monthly as part of the social security contribution or as a payroll tax. In this way, revenue could be obtained as a flow from the wages bill, but at the same time the tax could be identified with business taxation rather then sales taxation.

This is an important option which has not been extensively discussed. The combination of a payroll tax and a profits tax, rather than a VAT, could be a most attractive proposition to, say, the more left-wing political parties in Europe.

(e) As, theoretically, there is no distinction between the subtractive assessment of a VAT, $t (O - I)$, and the additive method, $t (W + P)$, then the EEC Commission could accept the principle of levying the VAT in either way. The point which convinced the EEC to adopt the VAT was the ease with which the tax content of sales prices could be assessed at any stage of production. It might be claimed that the additive method breaks the necessary link with sales and, therefore, the rebates on exports and balancing taxes on imports could not be known precisely. However, this would be sophistry. The two forms of levying the tax are identical. If the subtractive form was in fact absorbed, then the effects would be the same as the additive method when paid by the company. If the tax levied under the additive method were passed forward, it would have precisely the same effect as the subtractive method on sales passed forward.

If rebates are given to exporters under the EEC's subtractive base, there is no logical reason why the same rebate should not be given in a country where sales taxes are replaced by VAT levied under the additive method. Allowances for capital goods and stocks (see chapter 3) could be made identical against tax liability in both cases.

If the concept is accepted of an optional assessment of VAT by a combination of a proportional tax on wages and salaries (the payroll tax) and an annual (or possibly bi-annual) tax on profits, then the VAT becomes a much more flexible tax than it now appears.

However, taking all these considerations into account, the overwhelming, recurring theme, when discussing the EEC VAT, is the emphasis on the sales tax concept. The tax is *supposed* to be passed on to the consumer and should be seen to be passed on as a separate item on invoices right through to the final retail sales. The intention of encouraging the forward shifting of the tax is clearly shown in the help the French civil service gave to wholesalers and retailers in 1968 to calculate new prices 'while keeping the same profit margin.'[5] The Continental VAT is a charge, and is intended to be a charge on the consumer. If it is shifted backwards and absorbed by the firm, it becomes a tax on industry, services, distribution, etc. Therefore, the intention is to tax consumers; thus the tax fails if it is not passed on. If the intention were to tax businesses, this could be done more equitably by direct taxation (including a direct, additive, VAT). The one exception to this reasoning might be agriculture and this will be dealt with under that heading in chapter 4.

The subtractive method emphasizes the tax content of the sale and appears to tie the tax to sales. For this reason, it was chosen by the EEC.

Price inclusive or exclusive of tax

The next choice facing the EEC was whether to tax on a price inclusive, or exclusive, of tax. First, tax on a price inclusive of tax tends to conceal the tax element in the price. Second, it may complicate the public calculation of tax liability, as intrinsically it is more difficult to assess payments which are themselves part of the tax base, than to view them as quite independent of the tax base (see the example in Table 1.2). Third, the tax inclusive base creates the distinction between nominal and effective rates of tax. This distinction always understates the actual rate of tax to the consumer, and often produces odd rate percentages, as shown in Table 2.2.

[5] Rybczynski T. M., Ed: op.cit., p. 25.

On the other hand, the inclusive rate does simplify calculations of tax liability for the seller.

Most of the EEC countries decided to adopt the tax exclusive base, i.e., tax calculation exclusive of the 'tax levied under this tax'[6] and 'the taxable base is to constitute . . . all costs and taxes with the exception of the tax on value added itself.'[7] France still uses a tax inclusive base, but will, presumably, have to change. If the French VAT is treated as a cost by the retailer and passed forward entirely, it is reflected in higher prices. The inland revenue, by applying the nominal rates to the tax inclusive price to assess tax liability, forces the retailer, if he wishes to maintain his turnover unchanged net of tax, to apply a tax rate higher than the nominal rate. For instance, if the retailer decides he must net £100 to remain in business, a sales tax of 20% on a tax exclusive base would result in a selling price of £120 and a tax yield of £20. The tax base would be: £20/0·2 = £100. That is, the tax exclusive base leaves the retailer with £100 net. On the other hand, if as in France, he has a tax *inclusive* base, his selling price of £120 is taxed at 20%

Table 2.2
Nominal and effective rates of tax

French tax rates	Nominal %	7	15	19	25
	Effective %	7·53	17·65	23·45	33·33

and the tax yield is £24, leaving the retailer only £96. To ensure his net £100 he must now raise his selling price to £125; 20% of that leaves him £100. Thus the effective rate of tax becomes 25% although the nominal rate remains 20%. This is how the odd percentages occur in Table 2.2.

Note that the tax inclusive retail price is inflated to £125 and not £120, and the tax yield is increased to £25. To arrive at the correct tax base net of turnover tax, the rate should be the effective and not the nominal rate.

$$(\text{Tax base}) \ B = 25/0·25 = £100$$

The effective tax rate (t_e), is obtained from the nominal rate (t_n) by:

$$t_n = \frac{t_e}{1 - t_e}$$

$$t_e = \frac{t_n}{1 - t_n}$$

[6] Council of the EEC: Second Directive, 'On the Form and Methods of Application of the Common System of Taxation on Value-Added', *Journal Officiel des Communautes Europeenes*, No. 71, Brussels, 14 April 1967, Section 7 (i).

[7] International Bureau of Fiscal Documentation: *European Taxation: The Common System of Tax on Value Added*, Vol. 7, Nos. 7/8, Amsterdam, July/August 1967, p. 201.

This means that in France, the nominal rate of VAT is 25%, but the effective rate is actually 33·33%. (See Table 2.2.)

If we accept that the tax system should allow the customer to know his tax liability as simply as possible, then the tax on a price exclusive of tax is clearer, more honest, and less complicated than that levied on the tax inclusive base.

Direct and indirect methods

The third main decision was whether to assess tax liability by the direct or the indirect method. The direct method identifies the three main parts of the tax:

(a) Sales or output.
(b) Purchases or inputs.
(c) The difference between the two, or value added.

The normal way to assess any tax liability is first to calculate the amount taxable, and then to apply the tax rate to it, and this is what the direct method does.

The indirect method never actually calculates the value added, but only the tax liability. This requires the tax content of purchases to be shown on invoices so that it can be identified and subtracted from the sales tax content. This is sometimes referred to as the 'invoicing system of VAT'.[8]

However, the fundamental difference between the direct and indirect methods only occurs when more than one rate is used. This is best shown by an example.

In Table 2.3, example A, with one tax rate, is the same as the example in Table 1.1. Once more, the comparison is made by keeping the price excluding tax the same for each example and all taxation is on prices exclusive of tax.

In the single-rate tax example, the tax liability is the same under each of the three methods of calculation, direct addition, direct subtraction, and indirect subtraction. In the two-rate example (20% and 5%), the input of, say, electricity, is taxed at only 5%, compared to the normal rate of 20%. The tax on inputs is only £25 compared to £40 in example A. Yet the firm in example B is still liable for the full normal rate on its sales. This means that if the tax liability is calculated by the indirect subtractive method, subtracting the tax content of purchases (£25) from the tax liability on sales (£60), the tax to be paid is £35. But the firms *value added has not changed* from the first example; it is still adding £100, yet the tax liability jumps from £20 to £35. The direct subtractive method and, of course, the additive methods, would still give the old answer of tax liability at £20.

[8] Rybczynski T. M., Ed: op.cit., p. 45–46.

Table 2.3
Multi-rate VAT showing difference of direct and indirect methods of calculation

	A One rate				B Two rates				C Three rates			
	Price exclusive of tax	Tax rate %	Tax paid	Price inclusive of tax	Price exclusive of tax	Tax rate %	Tax paid	Price inclusive of tax	Price exclusive of tax	Tax rate %	Tax paid	Price inclusive of tax
Inputs:												
Raw materials	100	@20	20	120	100	20	20	120	50	20	10	60
Energy	100	@20	20	120	100	5	5	105	{50 / 100	10 / 5	5 / 5	55 / 105
	200			240	200			225	200			220
Value added:												
Wages and profit	100	@20	20	120	100	20	35	135	100	20	40	140
Outputs:	300	@20	60	360	300	20	60	360	300	20	60	360

(a) By direct addition:
  $T = t(W + P)$; 0·2 (100) = 20   (a) 0·2 (100) = 20   (a) 0·2 (100) = 20
(b) By direct subtraction
  $T = t(O − I)$; 0·2 (300−200) = 20   (b) 0·2 (300−200) = 20   (b) 0·2 (300−200) = 20
(c) By indirect subtraction
  $T = tO − tI$; 0·2 (300) − 0·2 (200)   (c) 0·2 (300) − 0·05 (100) − 0·2 (100)   (c) 0·2 (300) − 0·05 (100) − 0·10 (50) − 0·2 (50)
  = 60 − 40 = 20   = 60 − 5 − 20 = 35   = 60 − 5 − 5 − 10 = 40

Note: T = tax yield; t = the *relevant* tax rate; W = wages; P = profits; O = outputs; I = Input

With differential rates, the indirect subtractive method can throw the entire adjustment of tax from lower rates to the normal rate on to one firm. This is sometimes called the 'catching-up' effect. The same effect happens if three rates are used as in example C. Here two raw materials are supposed to have different tax contents of 20% and 10%, and energy remains taxed at 5%. The tax liability under the subtractive method jumps to £40, while the value added remains at £100, and hence the direct method of calculation still results in only a £20 tax liability.

The reverse also applies. If it happened that an input had a tax rate higher than the rate at which the stage following would be taxed, then the tax *relief* would be enjoyed entirely by the firm with the lower rate. This is still known as 'catching up'. (For a further discussion of 'catching up' see pages 62–67.)

The indirect subtractive method has the significant advantage of allowing the tax content of any sale to be known at once. It is always fully equivalent to the tax rate *at that stage of production*. This is extremely useful in a customs union using the destination principle of taxation (goods are taxed at the rates ruling in the country of destination) where numerous goods crossing frontiers have to be exempted from taxation as they are exported (and the tax rebated to the exporter), and then taxed by the importing country. This is the main reason why the indirect method was adopted by the EEC for, with differential rates, the tax content of any sale or purchase was fully known at every stage. Eventually, the EEC hopes to adopt the origin principle, (goods taxed at rates of the country of origin) simplifying the structure again, leaving only goods imported from countries outside the customs union to be taxed at the VAT rate appropriate to the manufacturing stage at which they are imported.

Another advantage of the indirect method is that in emphasizing the *sales* tax nature of the tax, it brings the VAT under the canopy of the GATT regulations on fair trade. Under the GATT rules, as a sales tax, it can be rebated; if levied as a *direct* tax on wages and profits, the GATT rules might not allow its deduction. One of the basic bones of contention between the US and the EEC is over how far the VAT allowance against exports under GATT favours European companies compared to US (and British) companies which can claim smaller sales tax exemptions and *cannot* claim rebates on taxes on profits and payrolls. Certainly the adoption of the indirect method of calculating VAT avoids this ambiguity.

It is significant that German complaints against France before the German change to the VAT, mentioned the 'virtual customs protection'[9] that the VAT gave France compared to other countries. This allegation was based on the very high rates at which the VAT was levied, compared to the cascade taxes of other countries, e.g., Germany at 4%, and the correspondingly low

[9] Schmölder, G: *Turnover Taxes*, International Bureau of Fiscal Documentation, Amsterdam, 1966, p. 71.

company taxes in France. Since the VAT could be rebated on exports, while other countries could not rebate their company taxes, France 'gives greater tax relief to its exports than its neighbours.[10]

The adoption of the VAT throughout the Community, although it still leaves the French levying higher rates and, therefore, claiming larger export rebates, at least allows every member to know the exact amount of sales tax that is rebated. But this still does not create equal treatment. Countries differ in their treatment of direct company taxes as well as in their sales taxes. All taxes on company expenditures, incomes, or sales, affect competition between companies. There are two solutions to this problem.

First, all taxes on businesses can qualify for equalization at tax frontiers. This would be equivalent to accepting the case put above, that a sales tax on wages and profits is equal to a tax on company value added. The main change would be to agree on a single proportional rate to apply to all sales, wages, and profits. Unless this were done, and different rates were applied to sales, wages, and profits, companies, if they absorb any of the taxes, would be penalized or favoured depending on their respective ratios of profits, wages, and sales. For instance, if profits and sales were taxed at high rates, while wages were taxed at lower rates, the low profit, low turn-over, labour intensive industry would be favoured.

Basically, the sort of change needed to implement this in Britain would be a replacement of the various purchase tax rates by a single proportional rate, say, 15%, and the same rate replacing the corporation profits tax and the SET. This rate, applied both to sales with credit offset for the rate on inputs and to wages and profits, would be equal to a VAT of 30%, i.e., $t(O - I) + t(W + P) = t(V/A) + t(V/A) = 2t(V/A)$. Therefore, this 30% could easily be rebated on exports at the border.

The assumption is, of course, that all these taxes are passed forward. As chapters 6, 7, and 8 explain, this is a large assumption, but no more misleading that that previously implied by the GATT terms whereby direct taxes on companies are assumed to be absorbed, while indirect ones are passed forward.

The second way in which all companies in different countries can contribute equally is to adopt the country-of-origin principle. That is, the place of production (origin) is the factor which determines equal tax liability. Every good produced in a country should be taxed equally regardless of where it is used, so that each product would reflect the taxes of the country of origin. This is in contrast to the destination principle where products are taxed equally according to their place of final sale (destination) regardless of their place of origin.

Clearly, the most usual principle today is that of destination. Normally, countries exempt exports from sales taxes and impose taxes on imports:

[10] Ibid.

that is, they operate to equalize according to where the product is to be sold —the destination principle.

The origin principle requires taxes to be levied on goods in the country where they are produced, even if they are to be exported. Taxes on exports appear against commonsense to most politicians. Such taxes are occasionally used as a convenient source of revenue from a staple export commodity, e.g., in Malaysia and Argentina, but, in general, exports are aided by tax exemptions rather than penalized by tax imposition. Probably the origin principle could only be adopted if a number of countries agreed to introduce it simultaneously. Theoretically, if all countries adopted the origin principle, then consumers could choose between domestically produced goods and imports according to the costs of production, including different taxes, in each country. Deficits or surpluses on the balance of trade would be corrected by changing the exchange rate (or changing factor rewards through deflation or inflation).

As world trade operates under a system of fixed exchange rates, such adjustments do not take place through exchange rate changes. However, if all countries in a customs union, such as the EEC, apply the same sales tax rate, then the tax liability is the same is it would be under the destination principle. Except for one most significant difference: the tax revenue under the origin principle accrues to the government in the country where the good is produced and not, as under the destination principle, to the government where the good happens to be sold.

From the point of view of the VAT system the tax revenue ought to accrue to the country where the value is added. This is what would happen under the origin principle. It does not happen at present under the destination principle. Under this principle, the country which exempts its exports from the VAT, automatically looses the revenue. This revenue accrues instead to the country that imports the good and imposes on them a VAT equal to the VAT borne by similar domestic goods. Thus, under the EEC's present destination principle, the VAT revenue on an exported product does not accrue to the government of the country where the value is added. This is why the eventual aim of the EEC is to adopt the origin principle between member countries. But at the same time as adopting the origin principle among themselves, they would apply the destination principle to countries outside the EEC. In this way, the EEC members would apply the same VAT rate in each country and the revenue from this would accrue to the government of the country where the good was produced. Exports from the EEC would be exempted from the VAT, but imports into the EEC would be liable to the standard rate of the VAT on similar goods, produced within the Community.

If the origin principle were adopted within the EEC, then company taxes could be equalized in the same way as the VAT and might also be rebated on products exported to countries outside the Community. In this way no concealed 'subsidy' to exports by sales or company taxes could be made between members.

Eventually, of course, this argument will lead to a discussion of the distorting role in final prices of taxes on factor incomes, particularly personal income taxes. Once more the logical action is likely to be an equalization of tax rates—but that lies beyond the scope of this book.

For the time being, the EEC is having enough difficulty in persuading all members to adopt the present VAT without the problem of changing to the origin principle. But the origin principle remains the long term aim for the structure of sales taxation within the EEC.

3. The tax base

Value added

The base on which the VAT is levied is peculiar. It is not what an economist would understand by 'value added'. The total value added of any country is recognized as the value of all work done within that country. If the value of replacing worn out capital goods is subtracted so that the value added becomes a figure showing the work done net of maintaining capital stocks, it is still not the same as the VAT base. The VAT base allows for capital certainly, but it allows for *all* new capital, not just that which replaces worn out capital.

Another difference between the national income form of value added and the VAT base is that usually exports represent work done but not available for domestic consumption but which, nevertheless, form part of national value added. Yet under the VAT system, exports are subtracted from the value added base. On the other hand, imports (which are nothing to do with domestic value added) are *added* to the VAT base.

The final complication is that government expenditure on wages and salaries is not part of the tax base and, therefore, government value added in this respect is omitted. Nor are certain services, e.g., doctors, lawyers, etc., included, although their work certainly adds to the national product.

So the VAT is not a tax on value added at all. It is a tax on domestic consumption in the private sector of the economy, but leaving out some services which are difficult to tax and which 'cannot readily be ascribed to the transaction'.[1] The easiest way to think of the VAT base is to consider it as a sales tax on most goods and services. If then, 'value added' is a misnomer, and the tax is in fact a sales tax, how is it different to a wholesale or retail sales tax?

The difference between a VAT and a retail sales tax, is that the VAT is 'fractionated', or collected in bits at each stage of production, which in total is equal to a tax on the retail sale at the same rate as the VAT. A 10% retail sales tax will have the same yield as a 10% VAT; only the 10% retail tax is

[1] National Economic Development Office: *Value Added Tax*, HMSO, London, 1969, p. 32.

collected in one lump and falls on one stage of production, whereas the VAT is collected in bits which add up to the full 10% on the final price.

So the tax base envisaged is extremely wide. It is specified as 'highly desirable to limit cases of exemption'.[2] The main types of exemption are three, those where goods and services are wholly exempted from tax; those where a zero rate is charged; and those on exports and imports. We will discuss them in that order. Afterwards, the treatment of the retail stage, the small business, government sales, and capital goods and stock will be considered.

Goods and services wholly exempted from tax

'The tax on value added shall be charged on:

(a) Deliveries of goods and the rendering of services, effected for a consideration within the country by a taxable person.
(b) The import of goods.'[3]

Under the normal exemption, the government gets the tax from all suppliers up to the exempt stage, while the exempt stage cannot claim any tax repayment. Thus, under the assumption that all VAT liabilities are fully passed forward, the exempted purchaser of the taxed inputs pays the tax but cannot claim a rebate from the government; so the burden of the tax falls on the exempt stage. To dramatize this position it is only necessary to think of a demand by farmers to be exempt from VAT to realize what that might mean. The farmers would pay tax on their inputs, yet because farmers were 'exempt', the public would not expect the price of farm output to rise. There would be pressure on farmers to absorb the tax liability and not pass forward fully the tax on inputs. In this way, the exemption becomes a tax on wages and profits at the exempt stage. The consequences of this for agriculture will be discussed in chapter 4.

But what is true for agriculture is true for all exempt stages. The exempt producer pays tax on his inputs and must either pass that tax forward fully, or absorb it. If it is absorbed, VAT ceases to be a sales tax and becomes a company tax. If it is passed on then, of course, it is immaterial to the producer whether he is in the scheme or outside it, but the VAT ceases to be neutral in two ways, first, it cascades, and second, it provides an incentive for vertical integration.

But it is generally agreed that VAT is ill-suited for taxing services connected with finance.[4] The value added by insurance companies or banks, for in-

[2] Council of the EEC: Second Directive, 'On the Form and Methods of Application of the Common System of Taxation on Value-Added', *Journal Officiel des Communautes Europeenes*, No. 71, Brussels, 14 April 1967.
[3] Ibid., p. 200.
[4] Committee on Turnover Taxation: *Report*, op.cit., para. 185.

stance, under the indirect subtractive method, would be difficult to calculate. The inputs could be considered as money deposits, but of course these would have no VAT content; the output could be repayments, but if these were taxed at the full VAT rate with no credit offset (because no VAT was credited on the input) clearly inequity would be created.

Looking at banking from the other end of the business, the trader who borrows from a bank considers the money as an input. But it would be difficult to tax all such borrowing or indeed to extend the VAT to all borrowing, including stock market flotations. The implication would be that when the money was repaid, a tax credit offset would have to be allowed. The only 'value added' to be taxed would be the interest paid on the loan.

The taxation of interest is a particularly awkward problem. At one extreme, you can argue that as money can be borrowed from private persons as well as from public institutions, and as VAT cannot be levied on the private person, the taxation of interest would put at a disadvantage the person who borrowed from a bank rather than from a friend; although hire purchase interest can be taxed under the VAT system. (See below.)

Alternatively, you can argue that loans are not the only thing the private person can provide. The distinction between the private person and the small trader can be very knife-edged. The housewife who makes dresses at home creates a value added which would be taxed in a shop. A do-it-yourself enthusiast performs numerous tasks which (with some allowance for inefficiency, family bad temper, and suspect workmanship) would be taxable if done by a normal trader. Why should interest be singled out for special treatment?

If banks were taxed, it would create two rates of interest (bank and private) and this might lead to an expansion of person to person borrowing; although essentially the amount of non-bank borrowing is likely to be minimal.

A more serious objection is the implication for other forms of borrowing. If a company raised money through the stock exchange either the issue would be liable for tax (and any redemption would create a tax credit), or the interest payment would be taxable. Of course the interest payment on an equity is the dividend, paid from earnings which themselves have already 'paid' the VAT. This could be held to be double taxation.

Life insurance companies would find themselves liable for tax on receipts, but without a claim until repayment. The long time involved could create difficulties during the transitional period (which would be protracted for this type of business) and might involve a heavy burden during an inflationary period.

Another objection to the taxing of financial services is the volume of transactions to be checked. One way to avoid this would be to assess the value added of financial services through the additive method by adding wages, salaries, and profits, and subtracting depreciation. This could be a neat solution. But to have the financial sector taxed under the direct additive method, and the rest of the economy under the indirect subtractive method might itself create inequity.

The usual way out of this difficulty is to exempt all such services as is the case in Germany and Denmark. A supplementary separate tax can be imposed on these services quite independent of the VAT. In France, the *taxe sur les activités financières* (TAF) at 13 % is levied on the profits of bankers, financiers, and generally on dealings in money and finance.[5] Taxpayers who are already taxed under the VAT structure are not required to pay TAF nor are local organizations, e.g., co-operatives who pay the local sales tax.

If it was decided to tax such activities in Britain, and a case can be made for doing so if most other services are taxed, then probably the most equitable way to do so would be by applying the VAT rate annually to wages, salaries, and profits, with deductions allowed for the depreciation of capital assets.

If it is decided not to tax financial services, then the implications are:

(a) All moneylending is excluded from the VAT.

(b) Stockbrokers and jobbers are excluded.

(c) Insurance companies in their insurance and investment business are excluded.

(d) As insurance investments are excluded from tax, 'insured persons will get no deduction for their premiums but will receive the claim moneys in non-taxable form. Hence when insuring stock in trade or business assets against fire it will only be necessary to insure up to 90 % of the value (with a 10 % VAT) as the assets insured would only realise 90 % if sold as the proceeds would be taxable'.[6]

These are substantial exemptions. It might pay governments to consider the possibility of taxing the value added of such businesses on an annual base of their wages and profits (the direct additive method).

The following is a good example of the cascade effect from exemptions:

There are both theoretical and real 'costs' involved in granting exemptions prior to the final taxable stage. Such exemptions run counter to the theoretical basis of a 'pure VAT' which levies tax only on the increment added to the value of a good or service. The effect of an exemption prior to the final stage, however, is accumulation of tax caused by including previously paid VAT in the base upon which a later VAT is applied. In short, there is a tax on a tax. An example of tax cumulation is provided by German law which specifically exempts the Government run post and telephone offices from paying VAT on sales of their services. Accordingly, these agencies may take no credit for VAT previously paid on sales of equipment,

[5] Frapsauce, M: *Comment Appliquer la Nouvelle T.V.A.*, J. Delmas et cie, Paris, 1968, S 1.

[6] Wheatcroft, G. S. A: 'Some Administrative Problems of an Added Value Tax', *British Tax Review*, September/October 1963, p. 354–5.

supplies and other factors of production to them; neither may they pass on a credit to those using their services. The result is a cumulation of tax: one paid on sales to the post office, which is borne by it and normally is reflected in the price of postal services; the other, paid by users of postal services on their subsequent sales, upon which no credit for any postal-related VAT is allowed.[7]

The other advantage of exemption, that of vertical integration, lies in absorbing the exempt stage. Suppose architects and surveyors were exempt from VAT. A builder would find it more sensible to provide his own architectural and surveying advice, thereby claiming exemption against their VAT liability. This would prove cheaper than employing outside firms who had to pay tax on their inputs and yet could claim no credit against them and, therefore, had to pass on the tax in higher prices.

The EEC Commission anticipated this possible encouragement to vertical integration (sometimes called the problem of 'captive goods') and declared that where a producer provides his own service which would otherwise be exempt, it is to be considered as a 'delivery' (delivery is the technical term determining the point of tax liability) and priced accordingly.[8] Clearly, the fewer internal services that have to be identified and priced the better so far as tax administration is concerned. But in Britain most industrial and commercial services would become liable to the VAT though most are not liable at present to any form of sales tax. Computer services, management analysis and advice, advertising, forwarding, etc., all enter as costs to registered enterprises and the VAT would be included in the final value of the retail sale, while no problem of captive goods arises.

The problem of exemptions is highlighted where the exempted producer can make a sale which is either an intermediate delivery, i.e., as an input for further production, or a final sale. Good examples of these are transport, telephones, stamps, and water.

Transport

Transport can be sold as a service either as a final sale, e.g., railway ticket for a schoolchild, or as an intermediate good, e.g., the same ticket bought by a businessman when travelling for his firm. If transport is exempt from VAT, the railway company will have paid tax on its inputs and presumably will pass forward this tax liability in the price of the ticket. Correctly, a schoolchild will bear the tax; but so will the firm of the businessman and the firm will be unable to claim that tax content against its tax liability.

In European VAT legislation, distinctions are drawn between the transport of goods and the transport of persons. In Denmark's original legislation,

[7] International Bureau of Fiscal Documentation, *European Taxation: The Common System of Tax on Value Added*, Vol. 7, Nos. 7/8, Amsterdam, July/August 1967, p. 188-9·
[8] Council of the EEC: *Second Directive*, op.cit., Article 5 (3) b.

all transport sales were liable to the VAT. Parliament amended these provisions and exempted the transport of persons. In Germany, although the transport of both goods and persons is taxable, a distinction is made for short 'commuter' journeys not longer than 50 kilometers. These are taxed at the low rate of 5·5 % compared to other transport sales at 11 %. In France, all transport sales are taxable.

As many forms of transport in Europe are state owned, at either national or local level, it would be easy to include, say, railways under the VAT system as their tax liability could be treated on an annual basis as a government bookkeeping entry. To avoid favouring some forms of transport vis-à-vis others, all transport should be taxed. Although there is at least one form of transport which is considered to represent so little competition it is not taxed—'transportation on waterways'.[9]

Theoretically, the purchase of the service provided by roads for private motorists should be taxable. The only 'purchase', however, is made when the annual road licence is bought. In a rough form, the licence represents a purchase of enough road on which to operate a vehicle. If he is not taxed, then the private road user has an advantage over the alternative taxed service provided by, say, a nationalized industry. This case is similar to the wireless/TV licence, . . . which is taxed in Denmark.[10] The basic position adopted in this book is to view these payments as a tax, and it would be illogical to impose a tax on a tax. The essential difference between the purchase of a road licence and, say, a railway ticket or postage stamp (which could also be considered as a tax if provided by a state monopoly) is that no variation in the quantity (or quality) of the service occurs with respect to price. The purchase of a road licence entitles the owner to use the road for one day in the year, or for every day, there is no change in the cost. But the purchase of a 3p stamp entitles the purchaser to post one letter; more letters require more stamps, thus resembling a sale rather than a tax.

Air transport retail sales are only liable to VAT if the journey is within the state. 'Taxable sales shall not include transportation of goods in this country direct to or from a foreign country.'[11]

Much the same reasoning applies to shipping as to air transport, except that the number of passengers carried domestically by shipping is negligible.

Telephones, telegraph, and telex

As explained above, the sale of these services by the Post Office has more the character of a genuine transaction than the sale of, say, licences. It is a matter for the state to decide whether to tax these services or not under the VAT structure, e.g., they are taxed in Denmark, but not in Germany. If they are not taxed, then the public's decision is between purchasing these

[9] Schmidt, H. K: *Added Value Tax Law: English-German Text*, Dr O. Schmidt, Köln, 1967, p. 37, sect. 4, (6a).
[10] Danish General Sales Tax: *Act No. 102*, March 1967, sect. 2m.
[11] Ibid., p. 9, sect. 12b.

untaxed services and others which are taxed. If, for instance, stamps were taxed and telephones were not, clearly there would be a benefit to those who relied on telephone conversations rather than letters; or if the option were to travel to see a person, or to speak to him by telephone, and one means of communication was taxed and the other was not, it would pay to use the untaxed service. More important than the internal equity would be the possible international inequity within a customs union if these services were not taxed in one country but were taxed in other countries within the union. Businesses which rely heavily on such means of communication, e.g., forwarding agents, would, in the country where such services were exempt, find their costs higher than competitors in countries where the tax was applied.

In general, it looks reasonable to include such items in the VAT structure. As they are provided by state agencies in most countries, their liability would be in the form of an internal government book entry. The British Post Office favoured using the zero rate to exempt it from the tax, but this option may no longer be possible as the EEC has specified that this rate should only be used as a transitional device.

Wireless and TV

The sale of licences for these services is taxed in Denmark but not in Germany. As argued above for road licences, it is better to treat these as a tax and not to levy a tax on tax. They are rarely used as inputs to business and, therefore, are best treated as exempt.

Water

The VAT legislation specifies water as a taxable item.[12] If it were to be taxed under a British VAT, it would be a considerable addition to retail values. In so far as firms must cover rates as a cost in their selling price, the cost of water is already included in retail values, but the private purchase of water is not within the tax base.

However, rates are most logically viewed as a tax and not as a charge levied for a service. 'We have no hesitation in rejecting the notion that rate payments are other than compulsory exactions, and in all subsequent discussions we treat them as a tax.'[13] To include water under the VAT structure would be to impose a tax on tax. Rates liability does not alter according to the amount of water used except in the case of industrial users. Possibly the best solution is to apply the VAT only to those users of water who are metered separately and charged in addition to their rates. This would ensure reasonable comparability between countries that levy block local taxes and those which are more closely tied to functional expenditures.

[12] Ibid., p. 1, sect. 2.1.
[13] Committee of Inquiry into the Impact of Rates on Households: *Report*, Cmnd 2582, HMSO, London, February 1965.

Houses, immovable property, and fixture installations

Immovable property presents a peculiar problem. It is an old and fascinating economic conundrum to ask what is the value of land and what is its reward? How would you assess the VAT liability of the sale of 100 acres of land in Lincolnshire?

The VAT is usually presented in the context of manufactured goods where stages of production are clearly defined. As land was not manufactured in the first place, the value added of land can only be related to its previous sale price. That is, the tax on value becomes a capital gains tax. This could be a neat way of taxing the sale of land for development. If agricultural land sales were not taxed, but sales of land for building were, then the state would be recouping part of the increase in value of development land.

The next difficulty is to assess whether a house and the land on which it stands can be separated. If only the sale of new houses is to be liable for the full tax on value added, and all development land sales were also liable, what would happen when an old house standing on a considerable acreage is sold? The acres might be sold off and used for development; under the above argument the sale of such land should be liable to tax, but the sale of the secondhand house should not. The difficulty is to allocate from the sale of the house and land, the value appropriate to the land. This could create another very awkward area for arbitration between government and private sellers.

The normal sale of houses poses few problems. New buildings, including houses, are liable to the VAT. Businesses, who buy factories, can claim offset for the VAT on the new premises against the VAT liability on their turnover. The purchaser of a house can claim no such offset.

This is straightforward. What is difficult is the question whether rent should be liable to VAT. A person renting accommodation, after the scheme had been in operation for a large number of years, will be paying a rent which compensates the owners for the cost of the house including their VAT payment. There would be no reason to make the rent payment itself liable to VAT. However, in a very long transitional phase, purchasers of new houses (who had to pay VAT) would be at a disadvantage compared to those who rented accommodation and whose rent did not have to cover the VAT. There is a further complication, that if an income tax assessment were made on the imputed rent of an owner occupier, e.g., the old British Schedule A, then if *that* were liable to VAT, the ordinary rent paid for rented accommodation would have to be liable to VAT.

Given the very emotional content of taxing accommodation, the best course is probably to apply the VAT to new houses and suffer the inequity of favouring those who rent old accommodation. As they are usually the poorer households, there is a possible progressive element in this. There is a possibility that, if new houses were liable to the VAT and people were renting accommodation which had not been liable to the VAT, the rents for the old houses might have to match the rent payable on new houses (which had paid the VAT). In this case, the economic rent implied by the extra payment that people would have to make on the old rented accommodation in order to match the new rent would favour the property owner, and probably operate in a regressive manner.

A final point in respect of building is the installation of fixtures. If the rate of VAT on the sale of the goods (fixtures) is different to that applicable to the building, then some definition has to be made of what constitutes 'building' and what 'installation of fixtures'. Of course, where the Swedish or Irish example is followed and a special reduction of the tax base creates a different rate for building, it is likely this will be different to rates on the sale of goods. Some rule which defines a portion of work as a percentage of the total installation is usual. So that, for instance, if under 25% of the cost of the installation is for wages and profits and over 75% for goods, then the transaction is defined as a sale of goods; if the value of the goods falls below 75%, then the rate appropriate to building is applied.

Medical services

Doctors' services, hospitals, and medicines are another controversial (and emotional) area of final sales. Taxation of medicines, surgical appliances, and hospital services always raises the public's hackles. The immediate emotional response to such taxation is that it is 'unfair' to tax health and thereby make it more difficult and expensive to regain good health (or to die). This will always be a good political platform. But this sort of redistribution (by not taxing 'vital' items important in low income budgets) is often found to be a highly regressive measure in practice. Instead of weighting consumer choice by differential taxes, it might be more equitable to help the consumption of particular goods and services through increased family incomes and transfers.

If medicines are exempt, then the typical stream of borderline cases emerges. Clearly, not all sales by chemists should be exempt. But when is a medicine not a medicine? Antibiotics clearly are medical, but so too is a glass of wine in certain circumstances. Medicines sold under prescription might be a form of safeguard for legislation. But the experience of the British Health Service in failing to check spiralling claims for medicines (which have been checked by the introduction of prescription charges) warns that doctors are not necessarily an effective substitute for pricing. American doctors have been known to prescribe a winter in Florida as a reasonable claim against income tax liability—how much more difficult then to check prescriptions for potent 'tonics'.

Most countries in the EEC tax medicine. More variable is their treatment of hospitals or homes for the aged. The VAT is not compulsorily applicable to the turnover of hospitals. This means that it is left to the discretion of each country whether or not it taxes such services. Hospitals on buying their buildings, plant, machinery, and equipment pay tax. This can be treated as the final sale, in which case the tax is paid by the hospital and is likely to be passed on to patients in higher prices. On the other hand, the hospital could be liable to the VAT and then claim the tax content of its purchases as an offset to its tax liability. Which system would benefit the hospitals more?

It might seem advantageous to exempt hospitals from VAT, but given that most hospitals are non-profit making institutions, if they absorb any part of the VAT, assessing them on their value added would amount to using wages as the tax base. If they were made liable to the VAT, then the offset of their tax liability on purchases could leave wages taxed if any of the VAT

Table 3.1

Possible tax liabilities of a taxable person (hospital), making no profit, with a 10% VAT, assuming the tax is absorbed

Position of the hospital under the VAT scheme	Inputs tax exclusive	Tax on inputs	Wages	Output tax exclusive	VAT liability	VAT net wages	Does it pay to be in the VAT scheme?
A (i) Not in VAT	100	10	50	150	10	40	Yes
(ii) in VAT	100	10	50	150	15–10	45	
B (i) Not in VAT	100	10	100	200	10	90	Immaterial
(ii) in VAT	100	10	100	200	20–10	90	
C (i) Not in VAT	100	10	200	300	10	190	No
(ii) in VAT	100	10	200	300	30–10	180	

was absorbed. The net balance of advantage depends on the size of the tax content of hospital purchases against the tax liability on value added, which in turn depends on the size of their value added. The lower the value added, the more it could be in the interest of a hospital to be a full part of the scheme. See Table 3.1 where the value added is assumed to be composed entirely of wages as the hospital is non-profit making. The hospital is assumed to absorb the VAT completely. If the hospital did not absorb the tax, but passed it on totally, it is immaterial to the hospital whether it is within the scheme or not.

Three situations are shown where wages are an increasing proportion of final output, £50 in A, £100 in B, and £200 in C. In each case, one row shows the hospital not in the full VAT scheme, e.g., A (i), and, therefore, liable for VAT on its inputs. The other row, e.g., A (ii), shows the hospital within the

VAT scheme paying tax on its inputs but able to offset this against the tax on its output.

It is assumed that the full effect of the tax is felt on wages. Thus, in example A (i), £10 is paid on inputs and this falls entirely on wages and reduces them to £40. If the £10 could be offset against VAT liability on output (£15), the net tax burden falls to £5 (15–10) and wages, net of tax, are £45. Clearly, it pays the hospital to be within the scheme.

When the proportion of wages rises to equal total inputs (example B) it is immaterial whether the hospital is within the scheme or not; the tax burden of £10 is the same.

Finally, when wages are larger than inputs (example C) the tax liability on value added (wages) is higher than that on inputs, and it pays the hospital to remain outside the scheme.

This is an interesting problem which clearly has implications wider than the case of hospitals. If, for instance, farmers absorbed their VAT liability and had the choice to be in or out of the scheme, the decision would depend on their proportion of profits and wages to inputs.

In general, a clear case for or against opting into the scheme cannot be made without first estimating whether the VAT will be passed on or not (if it is passed forward it is immaterial whether the person is taxed or not), and then estimating tax liability as the value added (wages and profits) changes as a proportion of total turnover.

Veterinary services

These might be considered as similar to those of doctors and other professional persons. But it can be argued that if agriculture is included in the VAT base—even if by a devious device (see chapter 4)—then veterinary services are not a final sale, but are a direct contribution to the cost of the final retail product, food. If farming is viewed in this way, vets would become liable to the full VAT.

There would be some inconsistency where vets dealt not with farmers' livestock but with the pets of the general public. In this case, the vet is not contributing directly to the cost of any final sale. However, since the proportion of veterinary services to farming far outweighs that to the general public, in most countries the inconsistency would be slight.

Entertainment

Many countries tax some sports but leave others untaxed. Denmark has followed this procedure under the VAT scheme. But it would seem more logical either to exempt all entertainment, as in France, or to tax it. There is little justification for favouring one type of entertainment more than another. The choice of some entertainments as more 'cultural' than others and, therefore, more deserving of preferential tax treatment must be invidious and lead to odd bed-fellows. For instance, in Germany, orchestras, theatres, parks, and zoos, are all exempt from VAT, while other entertainments, including sport, are taxable. Once more consumer choice ought not to be biased by this form of tax favouritism. If particular entertainments are to be favoured, it is probably more efficient to operate schemes of special direct grants which can be tailored more precisely to the needs of the enterprise and the intentions of the government.

Betting and gaming

On the Continent, betting and gaming are usually not taxed under the VAT. In Germany, betting is taxed separately and is exempted from the VAT. Where the state has a large interest in the betting agencies, e.g., the TOTE in Britain or France, it is easy to levy the VAT on an additive principle, i.e., wages and profits. But with private bookmakers, such an assessment is difficult. Perhaps a more simple alternative might be to levy a straightforward turnover tax on all betting and gaming as a roughly equivalent tax to the VAT.

Barter

Barter transactions are theoretically liable to VAT. The main difficulty is to check the value of such exchanges; the point is usually unimportant, but might be considered important in countries with large agricultural sectors where farmers absorb a substantial part of their own produce.

Auctioned and secondhand goods

It is difficult to know what the value added base is for auctioned and secondhand goods. A good entered for auction may have already paid tax when it was originally retailed. To treat the auction price as a second retail sale would be tantamount to taxing the good twice.

The actual value added of the acution is, of course, the auctioneer's margin and the seller's profit. To know this, the state would need to have the original invoice of the good when it was first retailed. Even then, in many cases there would be a negative value added as secondhand goods are likely to loose value through wear and tear. On the other hand, antiques would be expected to gain. If you treated the auction of antiques and houses which had gained in value from their previous sale as liable to the full VAT on the change in value, then the tax would be (as previously mentioned under housing) tantamount to a capital gains tax. If it was a capital gains tax then, theoretically, the state should also allow for capital losses, but this could be particularly embarrassing with secondhand goods where so many in fact would realize capital losses. It does look as though an effort to relate the auction price to the original first price would not be a useful device.

But if no tax is levied on the auction then clearly many sales will be represented as auctions and those conducting their transactions in this way would avoid tax compared to others who went through conventional channels. An obvious example would be the auctioning of fruit and vegetables in the wholesale market. But in practice, if auction sales were not liable to tax almost every sale could be represented as an auction sale. If two housewives bargained over the price of a carpet, this might be construed as an auction.

The solution lies in accepting only a limited number of registered auctioneers to be taxed under a special dispensation. This tax could be set at a special rate, quite separate from the normal VAT. It would apply only to goods which were clearly old and where there was a substantial time lapse between their original retail sale and the auction sale. Most antiques would be treated in this way. Any goods which were auctioned but which were clearly part of a continuing, current market process, e.g., fruit and vegetables, would have to be invoiced in the normal manner and a tax credit claimed.

There is a special difficulty in the sale of secondhand cars. Throughout Europe, cars are liable to high rates of sales tax; at the same time, it is common for cars to be sold secondhand between private persons as well as through official auctions and dealers. If VAT is liable on the secondhand sale through a registered dealer then it ought to be levied on the private sale, but this is administratively almost impossible. Alternatively, if the private sale is untaxed and the registered secondhand dealer has to pay VAT, then a substantial tax advantage is conferred on the private transaction.

This sort of discrepancy would not matter if the particular good were infrequently traded, or if it were of little value, or if the tax rate were low. But the combination of numerous sales, expensive items, and high tax rates, makes cars a crucial problem. If dealers have to pay a 30% VAT (the present purchase tax rate) whereas the private sale is tax free, the dealers' secondhand car trade collapses. This has proved a difficulty in every country (see chapter 10).

Another point to be noted especially with respect to cars is the definition of trade-in value. When a purchase consists of say 60% cash and a 40% allowance for a trade-in, the taxable consideration is limited to the 60% cash passing under that particular sale. Further VAT liability arises when the good traded-in is sold.

Other exemptions

There are a number of other minor exemptions or items where special provision has to be made. These include things like youth hostels and student lodgings which are not taxed under the VAT in Germany and France, but are taxed in Denmark. Theoretically, this could be held to bias a person's choice between untaxed youth hostels and taxed hotels, but the users of one are not easily switched to the other and the problem is unlikely to be large.

Works of art, antiques, and so on, are liable to tax, but the artist's sale of his own works is not liable to tax in Denmark, but it is in Germany and France. Artistry in any area is difficult to define and artists are all difficult to tax; the revenue authorities are often put in the awkward position of deciding when a piece of work is art and when it is not. The growth of multiple copies of works of art, e.g., lithographs, might almost be considered a factory process and, therefore, liable to tax. It probably is easier to try to tax all such work.

Other minor provisions can be made for sea-going vessels, internationally operated aircraft, the services provided on ships and aircraft, travellers' samples, etc.[14]

Partly exempt persons

It is quite possible for a person or firm to conduct both taxable and non-taxable business, e.g., a farmer might elect to be unregistered on his small farm yet also conduct a business selling agricultural machinery which would be liable to VAT. How do you apportion those purchases which will be allowable as offsets against VAT liability and those which will not? To insist that a particular say, capital good should be attached to a particular output may be impossible; for instance, how can you distinguish between a warehouse which contains varying quantities of taxed and non-taxed goods? Some rule-of-thumb definitions must be used. Probably the appropriate one is to allow current and capital inputs in the ratio of the proportion of sales taxed to sales untaxed over the year.

If this *pro rata* rule is adopted, there must also be some back-up rule on capital inputs to stop a person buying all his capital goods in a year when he has only taxable sales, thereby claiming 100% offset. In following years, the capital goods might be used to produce non-taxed goods and therefore the tax should not be totally offset. A messy solution, if this should be thought a sufficiently important problem, is to average the capital offset over a number of years, say, five or seven.

The zero rate

The zero rate is peculiar to the Netherlands and can be dealt with briefly.[15] For a transitional period, the Netherlands has decided to apply a zero rate of tax at the retail stage to socially necessary goods and exports. A reduced rate at the retail level passes the advantage entirely to the consumer. This naturally applies with a rate reduced to zero. The taxpayer, in this case, pays no tax.

The system is a technical device to operate a complete VAT structure while still exempting some commodities entirely from tax. To understand this device, the distinction between zero rate and the 'normal' exemption must be highlighted.

The zero rate is an actual *tax* rate of the VAT, the same as 25%, 10%, etc. Thus, the tax credit offset on purchases can be claimed against the tax liability, i.e., zero. On the other hand, a good which is exempt cannot claim

[14] NEDO: *Value Added Tax*, op.cit., p. 20.
[15] International Bureau of Fiscal Documentation: *European Taxation*, op.cit., p. 192–3.

any credit and has no tax liability against which to offset it and thereby pays tax on inputs which must be wholly passed on or absorbed.

In this way, the zero rate allows the consumer complete exemption because, for instance, the retailer can claim the full amount of tax he has paid on his input and, therefore, pays no tax, while all the previous stages have passed their tax liability fully forward. The government has gone through a complicated and administratively expensive procedure (collecting tax from all stages, and repaying it to the retailer) to get no revenue.

There is one neat use the Netherlands has made of her zero rate. Instead of exempting exports from tax as the official EEC directive requires, the Dutch tax the export at the zero rate. This exempts the export from VAT because 'the entrepreneur supplying the good or service on which the tax is imposed at a zero rate, receives a *de facto* exemption on the transaction and is entitled to a full credit or refund of the VAT previously paid since the transaction is formally subject to VAT and is not *stricto sensu* an exempt transaction'.[16] Export goods are those destined for direct transport to a destination outside the domestic territory (or to a bonded warehouse where the goods are registered as 'customs goods entered'). Similarly, 'customs goods entered' can be goods imported, and VAT payment can be delayed until the goods leave the warehouse and pass customs control.

However, in essence the Netherlands dearer rate on exports is simply a way of giving the normal VAT 100% export tax relief while technically keeping the export within the tax structure, i.e., tax at 0%. This is no different, except procedurally, from other EEC countries that rebate their exporters for the VAT content of their exports. Both systems involve the exporter showing the VAT content of the exported good—in the Netherlands, as a tax credit against VAT liability at 0%, in other countries, as a straight-forward claim against the state.

Exports and imports

Tax credits are allowed for the VAT embodied in all materials in goods exported. Exports are thereby free of tax when they cross a border. On entry to another country, as imports, they become liable to the full rate of VAT on similar goods domestically produced in the importing country. This import tax is levied on the full value of the import including carriage, insurance, freight, and customs duties. This treatment of exports and imports is that of the 'destination principle'.

Although under the VAT it is possible to know the precise VAT content of a good, nevertheless, border adjustment has given trouble. Under GATT the VAT is the only tax recognized as deductible on exports without involving subsidization. Yet it is clear that the more taxes are replaced by the VAT, the greater the amount the exporter will be able to reclaim, and the more

---

[16] International Bureau of Fiscal Documentation: *European Taxation: Netherlands*, November/December 1968, p. 287.

justified it is for other countries to maintain they do not allocate so many taxes to exporters and, therefore, they cannot subsidize exporters in the same way. The most obvious case is that of the tax on hydrocarbon oils. This is paid by industry in Britain, but it is impossible to recoup on the export of goods. If a hydrocarbon oil tax were replaced by a VAT and the tax recouped, the exporter would be put at an advantage compared to an exporter in another country who could not isolate the hydrocarbon oil tax content of his exports.

There is a flaw in this argument as will be discussed in chapters 6 and 7. In the micro-economic case, the exporter can be at an advantage the more tax he can isolate and claim as a refund on his goods at the border. In the macro-economic case, this is not necessarily true. The tax revenue lost by the government through giving tax relief on exports must be recouped elsewhere if the government is to maintain its revenue and expenditure. If recouped from, say, income tax, workers may claim a wage increase to compensate and thus increase costs, thereby making industry (including the exporter) less competitive. The export incentive argument for the exporter is taken at the micro-economic level in the case of the individual firm; at the macro-economic level, it is not necessarily as simple as it looks at first glance (see chapters 6 and 7).

The retail stage

In general, the fewer the exemptions the better for both taxpayer and government. However some exemptions must be made. The two main categories are retailers and financial services. It is generally agreed that small retailers (in Britain a suggested turnover of less than £5000 p.a.)[17] should be exempted or treated in some different manner. The administrative costs of collecting VAT from a barrow boy would easily outweigh the revenue, or any satisfaction from work well done in the revenue.

However, the EEC's directives envisage enforcing the VAT right through to the retail stage: 'The common system of tax on value added is to be applied up to and including the retail stage.'[18] But until tax rate harmonization takes place, members of the EEC are allowed to levy the VAT 'up to and including the wholesale trade stage, and then, where appropriate, to apply an independent complementary tax at the retail trade stage or at a stage prior thereto'.[19] A new directive proposes that the retail stage should be included in all countries by 1 January 1972.

This leaves a country four options:

(a) The VAT up to, and including, the wholesale stage, and a separate tax on the retail sale.

[17] Prest, A. R: 'A Value Added Tax Coupled with a Reduction of Taxes on Business Profits', *British Tax Review*, 1963, p. 9.
[18] Council of the EEC: *Second Directive*, op. cit., p. 198.
[19] Ibid., p. 298.

(b) The VAT up to, and including, the wholesale stage, and a separate additional wholesale tax and/or retail sales tax.

(c) The VAT up to, and including, the wholesale stage, and no further taxes applied.

(d) The full VAT up to, and including, the retail sale.

The first three of these options can all be used to avoid taxing retailers under the VAT.

Arguments against including the retail stage in the VAT centre on the difficulty of taxing businesses which may not keep the necessary records. It is not the number of outlets which is the core of the problem. although this is a factor. In France, there are over 1·5 million retailers liable to tax, compared to 277 000 liable for VAT levied up to the wholesale stage. Rather, it is felt that some countries with large numbers of retailers, many of them with small turnovers, sometimes ill-educated, and often unco-operative, should have the option of levying a simple turnover tax at a low rate instead of the more complicated VAT which requires the presentation of invoices and the calculation of the tax content of purchases.

Indeed, compared to the single-stage tax, e.g., the purchase tax, the exemption of small retailers under the VAT is easier, and costs the state less in lost revenue. As most of the tax will be collected at stages before the wholesale level, the cost to the government of exempting the retailer is only the tax on the retail value added. Of course, as the exempt retailer cannot claim credit on the tax content of his purchases, he will make his mark-up on a purchase price inclusive of tax, and this might involve a 'margin-on-tax' price increase.

Rather than exempt small retailers entirely, some flat rate charge or *forfait* (the French system of bilateral agreement on tax liability between the small taxpayer and the government) could be adopted. A sensible system might be one where a slightly penal flat rate was charged to encourage the retailer to keep accounts and to opt into the VAT structure.

But there are seven points against using a separate retail tax on top of the VAT up to and including the wholesale stage or exempting retailers entirely:

(a) It would be temporary in the EEC and would disappear as the VAT rates were harmonized.

(b) A flat rate turnover tax superimposed on the VAT has a cascade effect, unless complicated offsets are allowed, in which case it might as well be a VAT.

(c) If there is to be a multi-rate sales tax structure, it would be more useful to have the rates differentiated according to goods and services, instead of according to the outlets.

(d) With taxpayers who were both wholesalers and retailers, the Inland Revenue would have to impose some standard type of mark-up and this could cause inequity. The 'complementary' tax on wholesalers in addition to the VAT on a base roughly equivalent to the retail sale would assume a standard mark-up which reduces the neutrality of the tax and could penalize cut-price retail outlets.

(e) The separate retail sales tax would reduce the simplicity and neutrality of the VAT.

(f) Exemptions at the retail stage distort VAT neutrality. If the retail stage is exempted '. . . the relative price consideration of the final goods will be altered unless the costs of the final factor components form an identical percentage of all prices. If the prices of retail goods are distorted, and manufacturers purchase commodities from retailers, these distortions will enter into manufacturing pricing relationships'. Therefore, the EEC should 'insist that the tax be carried through the final retail trade stage'.[20]

(g) Retailers should be encouraged to keep accurate records of their dealings and not helped to maintain a slack procedure by a special dispensation.

In general, one of the main points in favour of the VAT is its homogeneity. As Germany, Denmark, and France have decided to apply the tax to the retail stage, except for special provisions for the very small retailer, it would be sensible for other countries to do so as well, if it would not cause too great an inconvenience. The Italians are to tax retailers separately with a Municipal Consumption Tax, but Italy has a highly fragmented sales tax structure which it would be unwise (to say the least) for others to copy.

The adoption of the VAT throughout the production and distribution chain avoids the awkwardness of a changeover at a later date. The calculations required of the shopkeeper are not too onerous and, of course, the keeping of such records has the incidental advantage of helping the Inland Revenue by cross-checking other tax liabilities.

The conclusion is that the complications created by introducing an equitable measure, which ought to be temporary, outweigh the minor advantages to the inefficient retailer.

Small businesses

Nevertheless, the very smallest producer (whether retail or at a stage before) should be given an alternative form of taxation to the VAT. The administrative cost savings of such exemptions are indicated in Germany and Denmark where exempting small businesses, annual receipts under £280 in Denmark, and under £1370 in Germany (see Table 3.2), reduced the number of taxpayers by a third.

The limits set by each country for complete exemption vary widely (see Table 3.2). Complete exemption treats small businesses as though they were

---

[20] Friedlaender, A. F: 'Indirect Taxes and Relative Prices', *Quarterly Journal of Economics*, February 1967, p. 134–139.

Table 3.2

Summary of the treatment of small businesses under the VAT system

	France	Germany	Belgium	Netherlands	Demark	Norway	Sweden
(a) Number of taxpaying small traders	1 100 000	636 500	—	—	—	—	168 000
(b) Number of retailers	1 100 000	402 000	—	100 000	60 000	—	150 000
(c) Limits for *complete* exemption	Tax liability £90 p.a.	Turnover £1370 p.a.	—	Tax liability £140 p.a.	Turnover £280 p.a.	Turnover £350 p.a.	Turnover £570 p.a.
(d) Special treatment for small businesses	Tax liability £900 p.a.	Turnover £6800 p.a.		Tax liability £206 p.a.			

consumers. That is, they do not need to keep records of their sales and their obligation to the state is limited to keeping their invoices in order. Of course, this means the government does not collect any revenue from the VAT which could be liable on the last stage. However the actual value added of a business with a turnover under £280 per annum (the limit in Denmark) would be so small that the administrative costs of collecting it would not be covered by the tax.

Germany and Denmark quote the exemption limit for businesses which are completely exempt from taxation on the basis of their turnover. France and the Netherlands quote it on the basis of tax liability. If businesses are to be completely exempt, that is if they are to buy inputs on which VAT has been paid but against which they cannot claim any credit, i.e., they are to be treated more or less as a final consumer, then it seems more sensible to exempt them on the basis of turnover rather than tax liability. After all, why go to the trouble of working out the business tax liability if the firm is then to be exempted? Administratively, it is neater to use the figure for turnover.

Whether or not tax liability or turnover is used as the exemption point, the striking feature of the Continental treatment is the variability of the definition. A turnover under £1370 a year in Germany allows complete exemption, whereas a turnover almost one-fifth of that at under £280 per annum is the qualifying level for Denmark. Norway and Sweden have turnover limits within that range. The same sort of variability is shown if tax liability is taken as the qualifying limit: in France, the tax liability must be under £90 a year, whereas in the Netherlands, it must be under £140 a year.

Clearly, if there is to be harmonization not only of the rates of the VAT, but also of the structure in various countries, then considerable problems of definition need to be ironed out. To get comparability between countries as diverse as Germany and Norway will require a considerable amount of adjustment on the part of every country. Basically, the bigger industrialized countries will find it more profitable in terms of administrative efficiency to make their exemptions high rather than low. On the other hand, more agricultural communities, and those with many small craft industries, cannot afford the lost revenue which would be involved if large numbers of small businesses were exempted.

The more industrialized countries also combine their treatment of completely exempt businesses with an intermediate stage before the normal VAT structure applies, of businesses which are neither small nor sufficiently large to be completely within the normal structure. This is shown in Table 3.2(d), under the special treatment for small businesses. These are traders who can opt for a more simplified tax form and a less frequent period of payment (see also pp. 155–159).

Once more, smaller, more agricultural countries do not see the need for this refinement. It is interesting that the Netherlands, which is the smallest of the three countries to have adopted this intermediate stage, has a very narrow band between the £140 p.a. exemption limit for the completely exempt business, and £206 p.a. tax liability as the top limit for the special treatment for small businesses. France, however has adopted an extremely wide band from £90 p.a. tax liability for the top of the completely exempt businesses up to £900 p.a. for the special treatment for small businesses. This means that although special treatment is meted out to a large number of small businesses and craft industries in this category, they do not, like those who are completely exempt, escape the tax net completely.

It pays to extend the tax, as far as is reasonable, to every taxable person. If the business is small, the tax should be so arranged that a penalty is involved if the person is unable, or unwilling, to keep adequate records to allow assessment under the VAT. Where assessment is impossible on a monthly basis, an annual assessment using the additive method could be allowed.

Government

There is no reason why government should pay the VAT. To pay the tax would involve a great increase in work simply to achieve a transfer of funds.

Although neither central nor local government should pay the tax, nationalized industries ought to be liable. As argued above, if nationalized industries are in competition with other industries, then both industries should be liable under the same tax structure to ensure that competition is not biased by taxes.

Finally, many government agencies buy buildings. Indeed half the new construction in Britain is bought by such bodies. These government agencies would have to pay the VAT on the new buildings, but would be unable to offset this tax liability against any sale. This would raise the price of such building to the government compared to other businesses. The government might forego the tax on such a sale to a government agency, at the same time reducing the price paid. But, of course, contract prices would soon be set by the construction industry to allow for such adjustments. Probably the least messy solution would be for the government to pay the VAT embodied in the cost of a building. It is an awkward solution to an awkward problem.

Capital goods

The VAT is designed to exempt goods used in the production of further goods. It is intended to fall on final sales only.

There are two ways in which capital goods can be treated. First, the full value of the VAT embodied in the good can be allowed as an offset against current VAT liability. This has the great advantage of simplicity. It means no elaborate records of capital depreciation must be kept by the authorities. But it does mean that substantial capital purchases could create a large claim on the state far in excess of current VAT liability. The option is then open to the state to repay the claim in full at once—which clearly would give the maximum encouragement to capital creation. Alternatively, the state could allow the tax credit to be carried forward indefinitely until cancelled by tax liabilities (which must happen unless the firm goes broke). Or the state could allow the debt to roll forward for a set maximum time, and then pay it in full. Or the state could repay some maximum amount each tax period. All these variations are used (or proposed) within the EEC.

The second way of treating capital goods is to specify some pattern of depreciation and allow the appropriate tax content of the capital sum to be deducted each tax period. This suffers from numerous disadvantages especially where, as with buildings, depreciation could be spread over twenty years. It is not a method used by anyone in the EEC.

Further problems of the treatment of capital goods will be found in chapters 6, 7, 8, and 9.

Miscellaneous problems, credit, discount, bad debts, containers, hire purchase

There are at least five further problems worth mentioning:

(a) **Credit.** The invoice is the crucial document in the VAT structure and it is on the invoice that VAT is liable. But firms may receive the actual cash for the sale many months later. Thus VAT may have to be paid before cash is received. The larger the value added and the more extended the credit period, the bigger the problem. Essentially, this is a once and for all transitional problem of extending company finance which is not unique to the VAT. Every time sales taxes are increased, firms with credit extentions longer than that which the tax authorities extend to them, have to find the extra finance. Moreover, the problem only affects companies which do not already pay tax. As Continental countries had operated cascade taxes which had fallen on every stage in the production process, there was no abrupt change of principle. There would be an extension of the tax base in Britain.

(b) **Discount.** Many firms sell items at an invoiced price which may be adjusted for prompt payment or for further bulk orders. The VAT should fall only on the actual value added even though the record of the invoices may be different. This can be met by a system of annual reconciliation. It should be noted that unless the final retail sale changes, the total value added has not changed and therefore, there should be no change in the total VAT liability. It is only a question of re-allocating liability between firms and this is probably unimportant especially if the tax is fully passed on (see chapters 6 and 7).

(c) **Bad debts.** A similar problem occurs with bad debts. A business may have invoiced sales, but been unable to collect the cash. Once more, to avoid inequity, there should be an annual reconciliation.

(d) Containers. A further example of a difference between invoice and final cash received is when containers, or other returnable items, e.g., pallets, are returned. If a reconciliation is not allowed on the final retail sale, then excess VAT may have been collected.

(e) Hire purchase. Finally, not only the hire purchase sale of a good may be liable to VAT but also the element of interest included in the down payments and successive payments. As other financial services are not taxed, this could be held to be discriminatory. But if hire purchase transactions clearly show the price and the interest payments separately, presumably the VAT could be collected on the sale of the good only.

4. The value added tax and agriculture

The reasons for taxing farmers

The treatment of agriculture is a special case of exemption. Agriculture in the EEC is to be taxed indirectly and this involves a type of exemption. So while some comments appear to suggest that agriculture is exempt, nevertheless it still ends up taxed. Such an apparently contradictory treatment merits a chapter to itself.

The EEC proposes to extend the VAT to agriculture to complete the tax base. This is held to be in the farmers' interest as farmers would be penalized if they were left out of the scheme. This is sometimes difficult to explain, but is important.

A farmer, exempted from paying VAT cannot claim credit for his tax liability on his purchases. So he pays tax on his inputs and cannot claim an offset. That is, he has a net liability. Of course, if all taxes are passed forward, the farmer will simply pass on the tax content of his purchases; but then because the purchaser cannot take credit for the tax passed on to him, the total tax content rises and a cascade is introduced. The farmer's sale will include all the VAT he has paid on his inputs, but the purchaser cannot claim the VAT paid as a credit on his inputs because the 'chain' of the VAT has been broken. This means that when a food processer sells his output, having added value to his purchases from the farmer, he is liable to VAT on values which already include VAT, and this is a cascade. Thus, when farmers are exempt, if the VAT is absorbed, it is an unfair tax on the farmers, if passed on, a cascade.

For these reasons, the VAT should be extended to agriculture. However, it is not proposed by the EEC to apply the same type of VAT (indirect subtractive) as that applied to other goods and services. The main reason for changing the system in regard to agriculture is that so many farmers are small producers and are often unable (and unwilling) to keep the accounts necessary for full VAT calculations. It is argued that because farmers do not keep such accounts, they should have special treatment. Of course, it could equally well be argued that since the keeping of accounts should improve farm efficiency (and incidentally often provide governments with an otherwise unobtainable figure for farm costs, sales, and profits) the VAT provides the ideal mechanism to encourage the keeping of farm accounts. This point will be returned to later. Other points about the VAT and farming are made in chapter 10.

The EEC method of taxing farmers

To create a system which would be easy to operate, the Commission of the EEC has suggested two main provisions: first, a flat rate 'global credit offset', and second, a common low tax rate, 'deliveries and imports of listed goods shall be liable to the value added tax at the common reduced rate of "x%".'[1] This means farmers will not have to keep invoices for purchases, or be involved in tax payment at all.

The *purchaser* of farm output, who is fully accountable for tax, will be liable for the farmer's VAT, and for the VAT on his own value added. That is, the two stages:

(a) The farmer or agricultural producer and
(b) The purchaser of farm output

are rolled into one, and it is the purchaser who takes care of the tax liability for both.

Thus we have two stages and three tax rates:

First rate: the normal VAT rate of, say, 20%, which the farmer pays when he buys his raw materials (inputs).

Second rate: the global offset credit which *theoretically* should give the equivalent of the tax paid by the farmer on his inputs; that is, it should be the same as the 20% on raw materials mentioned above. In this example, the credit rate is fixed at 5%.

Third rate: the special reduced rate of tax for agricultural output, in this example 10%.

Table 4.1 shows the position. There are two stages where value added is created—farming and then the purchaser from the farmer. We have two sales, one by the farmer of his output (£300), the other by the purchaser of farm output (£440 tax included).

The calculation:

(a) Global credit offset: £300 @ 5% = £15.
(b) Tax liability of the purchaser of farm output on his *purchase* from the farmer at the reduced rate of tax on agricultural products with the credit offset subtracted: £300 @ (10% @ 5%) = £15.

[1] Council of the EEC: Proposed Third Directive, *Terms and Conditions for the Common Application of the Tax on Value Added to Operations Related to Agricutural Products*, Brussels, February 1968.

(c) Final tax liability of purchaser of farm output: £400 @ 10% = £40, minus £15 from (a) above = £25.

The farmer has bought raw material inputs (£75) on which he has had to pay VAT at the normal rate of 20% and, therefore, his tax liability on this first transaction is £15. If the farmer was a full member of the VAT structure, he would compute his total tax liability by subtracting his tax paid on inputs from his tax liability on his sales at the special low agricultural VAT rate of 10%, this would be £28·5 minus £15. However, the farmer does not calculate any VAT liability but simply sells his full output, including of course the VAT paid by him on his inputs, at the final selling price of £300. It is most

Table 4.1
Computations to assess agricultural VAT liability

		Price exclusive of tax	Tax	Price inclusive of tax
Farmer	Inputs	75	15	90
	Value added	210	—	210
	Output	285	15	300*
Purchaser of farm output	Inputs	285	15	300
	Value added	115	25	140
	Output	400	40	440

* *Note:* This is the only figure known for the farmer. Both credit for the VAT on inputs (a) and his theoretical tax liability (b), are calculated from it.

important to realize that the farmer's output (£300) is the only *known* figure; his value added, his inputs, and the tax content of his inputs are all subsumed in his final price.

When the producer buys the farmer's output (£300) he 'draws up two copies of a purchasing document,'[2] showing the price before tax, £300, and the proportion of tax due by the agricultural producer on his purchases of inputs which is estimated by the special rate of the global credit offset, in this example, 5%, that is £15 ((a) in Table 4.2). One copy of this document is given to the farmer and the other is countersigned by the farmer and retained by the purchaser of the farm output.[3]

The *purchaser* of the farm output is then liable to pay VAT at the agricultural rate minus the global offset rate (10%–5%) ((b) in Table 4.2)[4] that is, £300 at 5% = £15. Thus, the purchaser's theoretical, immediate tax

[2] Ibid., Art., 7: 3 (a).
[3] Ibid., Art., 7: 3 (c).
[4] Ibid., Art., 7: 3 (c).

liability is £15. It is theoretical because, in fact, he does not actually pay this sum to the government, but sets it off against his final tax liability on his own sales.

The final tax liability of the purchaser comprises the agricultural tax rate at 10% on his final sale at a tax exclusive price. (This is in accordance with the VAT legislation in all countries except France and Sweden where it is inclusive of tax. This final sale is compounded of his inputs £285, and the value he added to those inputs £115, making £400 in all, and a tax liability of £40. ((c) in Table 4.2.)

Against this he can offset two things:

(a) The amount of tax theoretically paid by the farmer on his inputs and shown on the document countersigned by the farmer . . . £15 ((a) in Table 4.2).
(b) The amount of tax the purchaser has already *theoretically* paid ((d) in Table 4.2) but by offsetting at this stage he negates the tax liability.

Thus the purchaser is the only one who has any dealings with the government. The farmer never makes any returns to the government. The purchaser's total dealings with the government are:

Table 4.2

VAT liability of the purchaser of farm output

	Credit £	Liability £
Tax liability of purchaser of farm output (b)		15
Tax liability on own final sale (c)		40
Credit for global offset (a)	15	
Credit for tax liability of farmer (d)	15	
	30	55
Net liability of purchaser		25

This rather complicated way of achieving agricultural tax liability is laid out in the official EEC Directive; but it can be greatly simplified. Note that items (b) and (d) in Table 4.2 are selfcancelling and, in fact, the purchaser never actually pays (b) to the government but simply offsets (d) against it. Thus to calculate the total tax liability of the two stages, all that needs to be done is to subtract (a) from (c) in Table 4.2. That is, the purchaser of farm output will simply apply the agricultural tax rate (10%) to his output (£400) and subtract from the £40 tax liability the tax content shown on the document countersigned by the farmer (£15); this gives a net tax liability of £25 for the purchaser.

Note that the government's tax revenue from these two stages is £40, £15 on the farmer's inputs and £25 from the purchaser of farm output (£15 + £25). If the VAT were calculated in the normal way by the indirect subtractive method, with the farmer a full member of the scheme, the tax collected by the government would be 10% on the farmer's tax exclusive output of £285, that is £28·5 with the tax on his inputs subtracted, £15, giving a net tax liability of £13·5. The purchaser would be liable to 10% on his sales, £40, with 10% on his inputs subtracted, £28·5, making a tax liability of £11·5. Thus with the £15 the farmer paid on his inputs, the total government revenue would be £40 (£15 + £13·5 + £11·5), exactly what it is using the more roundabout way devised by the EEC to circumvent the farmer (and it is clear this is the intention from the preamble of the Third Directive).

What has happened is that the 'catching-up' process occurs at the second stage under the EEC scheme and so the final total tax liability remains the same, but the farmer's value added, £210, is untaxed, and the purchaser's value added of £115 is taxed by £25.

This is the perfect solution in theory; in practice, it is most unlikely that the relative rates of the common low agricultural tax rate, and the global credit offset, will be set in such a way as to produce the results described above. There are two influences which disturb this happy solution:

(a) The flat rate global offset.
(b) The common reduced rate for agricultural products.

The flat rate global offset

This is the rate which is applied to the farmer's output to estimate the VAT content on his purchases of raw materials. There are three main points about the flat rate global offset; first, its effect on the farmer's efficiency; second, its use as a subsidy; and third, its use to determine the farmer's value added. The exact rate of offset chosen is most important.

> With the macro-economic data available serving as a basis, this rate will be determined in such a way that global adjustment can be assured for the offsettable tax on value added weighing on the purchases made by all farmers coming under the flat rate deduction arrangement, and on the services rendered to them.[5]

The most important point here is that such a global offset cannot be correct for all farmers (unless all farmers have precisely the same input patterns, relative values, and efficiency). If one farmer is more efficient than another, e.g., he produces the same output with a relatively smaller input, his global offset will be the same because it must be related to the sale price, which will be the same for the efficient and the inefficient farmer.

[5] Commission of the European Communities: *Proposal for a Directive on Application of the Tax on Value Added to Turnover in Agricultural Products*, Spokesman's Group: Press Release, 23 February 1968.

Table 4.3

The advantages to a farmer of increased efficiency under VAT

(£)

	A			B			C		
	Price excluding Tax	Tax	Price including tax	Price excluding tax	Tax	Price including tax	Price excluding tax	Tax	Price including tax
Inputs	75	15	90	50	10	60	100	20	120
Value added	210		210	240		240	180		180
Output	285		300*	290		300*	280		300*

* For VAT purposes it is important to remember this is the only known figure.

In Table 4.3, example A is the same as that used previously, only in this case the reader should imagine a buyer of £300 worth of goods from the farmer. This is the only price known in the market; the farm purchases and value added of the farmer remain known to the farmer only. In example A the farmer's value added, after passing the tax forward, is £210; in example B it rises to £240, which is more than his increased efficiency in economizing on inputs justifies (reduced by £25 from £75 to £50). The improvement in the farmer's value added (by £30) is partly due to his improved efficiency (£25), but helped by his lower tax liability on inputs (£5). Thus, if the farmer becomes more efficient and lowers the cost of his inputs (B) yet maintains his selling price at £300 (which is quite likely in agriculture where many selling prices are guaranteed), he gains a tax advantage. Therefore, this global credit offset encourages efficiency.

The reverse is also true. Inefficiency and high inputs for the same output reduce the value added in C by £30 compared to A, and this is more than the rise in the cost of inputs to the farmer (£25). The deterioration in value added by £30 is partly due to the higher inputs (£25), but increased by another £5 of VAT. In this way inefficiency is penalized.

A further point about the credit offset is that it can be used as a subsidy to the farmer. If the offset is set at a level much higher than the likely tax content of farm inputs, then farmers and/or purchasers of farm output would be subsidized to that extent. To imagine an extreme case, if provision was made for an offset exactly equivalent to the actual VAT liability on farm inputs, then the farming stage bears no VAT at all. In Table 4.4, example A is the same as shown in Table 4.1, and the tax on value added for the two stages is paid by the purchaser. (Throughout these examples the inputs of the farmers remain the same, as does the selling price of the purchaser of farm output; the agricultural tax rate is kept at 10%.)

In example B, the credit offset is increased from 5% to 10% and the value of the offset rises from £15 to £30; the farmer's position is unaltered, but the tax free value added of the purchaser, i.e., wages and profits, rises from £115 to £130 and his VAT liability falls from £25 to £10. Of course this 'subsidy' to agriculture need not accrue to the purchaser of farm output. It could accrue to the farmer, or be split between the purchaser and the farmer.

In example C, the credit offset is again fixed at the high rate of 10%, but this time the farmer increases his selling price to £310 and his value added (untaxed) rises by £10 to £220. The purchaser of farm output is still better off than he was in example A with an untaxed value added of £121 compared to £115 in A. So in example C, there is a subsidy to both parties when the credit offset is raised, by the farmer having the power to increase his price to the purchaser of farm output.

Again the reverse is true. If the global credit offset is fixed at a level below the normal tax content of farm purchases, then a tax penalty is created. In example D, the credit offset is reduced to 3% (from 5% in example A).

Table 4.4

Farming subsidies and penalties under the VAT

		A Initial position, no advantage			B Credit offset increased, advantage to the purchaser			C Credit offset increased, advantage to both			D Credit offset decreased, purchaser penalized		
		Price net of tax	Tax	Price with tax	Price net of tax	Tax	Price with tax	Price net of tax	Tax	Price with tax	Price net of tax	Tax	Price with tax
Farmer	Inputs	75	15	90	75	15	90	75	15	90	75	15	90
	Value added	210	—	210	210	—	210	220	—	220	210	—	210
	Output	285	15	300	285	15	300	295	15	310	285	15	300
Purchaser from the farmer	Inputs	285	15	300	270	30	300	279	31	310	291	9	300
	Value added	115	25	140	130	10	140	121	9	130	109	31	140
	Output	400	40	440	400	40	440	400	40	440	400	40	440

This increases the tax on the purchaser from £25 to £31 and his net value added falls from £115 to £109. Again this penalty could be spread between the farmer and the purchaser. Given that in agricultural markets farmers are numerous, individual sellers who are not well organized for joint selling, and the purchasers of farm output are relatively few, the likelihood is that any penalty from a low rate of credit offset would be pushed back to the farmer.

If the government wanted to encourage farmers to join the full VAT structure, then it would pay the government to fix the offset at a low level. The farmer could then compare his liability for VAT under the present system to what it would be if he joined the full scheme, and the temptation should be to join the full VAT structure.

The EEC Commission provides that 'every farmer is to be free to opt for application of the normal tax on value added'. If farmers were persuaded, perhaps by an offset fixed at a low rate, to join the full VAT structure, it would carry the attendant benefits of:

(a) Ensuring the tax as a real tax on the farmer's value added and not on a fictitious figure.
(b) Involving the farmer in the tax structure.
(c) Encouraging the farmer to keep accurate accounts (just like businesses). Once a farmer was in the VAT structure, it would be in his interests to make sure all invoices were returned.
(d) Providing information on farm inputs, outputs, and income. These are considerable advantages. They are particularly valuable in countries where farmers' profits are traditionally undervalued (France) or not taxed at all (Ireland).

The more sophisticated the farming, the more it pays the farmer to participate fully in the VAT structure. In Denmark, where farming is highly mechanized, the tax credits on the expensive inputs were so important to farmers that they chose to be included in the new tax. With the 'bunched' payments and receipts of many farmers, it is probably best to collect the tax not on a monthly basis, but rather related to the main receipts (harvest) time. In Denmark, for instance, the VAT is paid twice a year.

In the examples in Table 4.1, the farmer's value added was not taxed. The complete 'catching up' took place at the succeeding stage. If this is how the tax works in practice, clearly it is unfair. However, presumably the purchasers of farm output will try to pass some of their tax liability back to the farmer by cutting his value added through pushing his selling prices down. This could be a difficult time, when middlemen try to push farm prices down and, at the same time, the farmer knows he is paying VAT on his inputs. It will also be awkward to explain to a farmer, who is signing a document showing the claim the middleman can make on the farmer's selling price (the credit offset), that he is not to share a part of this claim. Farmers will almost certainly view such a situation with suspicion.

The global offset clearly offers a temptation to countries competing in a customs union to subsidize the agricultural producer. To help avoid this, the EEC Commission has suggested a second major provision in addition to the common global offset, a common tax rate.

The common low agricultural VAT rate

This single agricultural tax rate throughout the Community is set at 'half the arithmetic mean of the normal rates of tax on value added to be applied in the Member States on 1 January 1970 serving as a basis'.[6] This still makes the rate about 7%. However, as the obligatory single agricultural rate applies only up to and including the wholesale stage, the final rate to the consumer can be adjusted at the retail stage.

The term 'agriculture' includes all producers engaged in agriculture, forestry, fishing, fish farming, oyster cultivation, etc. Of course, a rate of 7% on food in Britain would be unprecedented, but the *principle* of taxing food has already been accepted in most European countries. Even if a 'normal' high rate of tax were applied to agricultural producers, this could be ameliorated by a special low rate at the retail level.

Another way to reduce the tax content of food would be to zero rate farmers. That is, they would be able to claim from the government all the tax they paid on inputs against a zero tax liability. This would mean that all farmers would have to be fully registered VAT payers, and they would have to keep records of all their invoices on purchases.

An alternative, which would avoid pulling farmers into the VAT net (at least until obliged to do so by the EEC Commission), would be to zero rate main agricultural inputs. But this creates its own difficulties which may be little appreciated at the superficial level. There are few agricultural inputs which are so specialized and unique to farming that they can be ascribed only to agriculture. Obviously fertilizers, tractors, and buildings have uses other than farming. But even something so apparently specialized as a milking machine is really only a plumbing job involving a number of engineering products which could quite easily be used for something different.

As mentioned in the section on exemptions, food provides one of the best examples of a range of goods which can be taxed conveniently at a lower rate. Food does not provide the inputs for a large number of other industries. Most of it is processed vertically straight to the consumer, therefore, the costings of many other industries will not be upset by the 'catching-up' mechanism.

On the other hand, 'agricultural products' such as wool, hides, etc., do form a significant input to industry, and such industrial users could become the victims of 'catching up' if the tax rate on agricultural products was

[6] Commission of the European Communities: *Proposal for a Directive on Application of the Tax on Value Added to Turnover in Agricultural Products*, Spokesman's Group: Press Release, 23 February 1968.

significantly lower than the rate on other products. This provides a strong reason for levying the full 'normal' rate on agricultural producers. It avoids large adjustments in firms using agricultural products as raw materials. If relief from the normal rate is wanted for food, then it can be given at the retail level by a special low retail rate.

Generally, as farmers will eventually have to be part of a full European VAT structure, it is probably better to pull them in at the beginning and adjust the tax content of food by zero rating at the farm or retail level.

Agricultural exports

The common tax rate reduces the formalities of tax adjustment on agricultural goods at customs frontiers within a customs union. Within the EEC, there will be no refunds on the export of agricultural goods, the tax will simply be collected from the first buyer after importation.[7]

The need to avoid VAT rebates on agricultural exports is underlined if the possibility of treating exports of agricultural products like any other exports is considered; that is, the exporter would be able to claim a rebate for the full amount of the VAT in the good exported. Now this treatment is reasonable where the exporters are few, the exports clearly identifiable, and where the goods are difficult to import or export except through a limited number of clearly recognized points of entry or exit.

If the exporter were a farmer, he could claim the credit offset on his export price. If the exporter were a middleman, he could claim the low agricultural rate. In both cases, the exports would be difficult to identify. It is reasonable to have an identification number on a car or refrigerator, something similar can be done with cattle, it becomes more difficult with pigs and sheep, and completely unreasonable with hens, eggs, and cabbages. If the goods cannot be identified, if the persons involved in the trade are numerous, and if there exists a possibility of re-importing the goods illegally, then governments could have a large problem on their hands.

If a farmer exports, for example, his sheep and claims the rebate, then secretly gets the same sheep (or indeed *any* sheep) back across the international border, he can re-export the animals and claim the rebate again. Every time the agricultural produce is exported, the rebate is claimed. The produce might never actually have to change owners as long as it passed through the border on a nominal sale to claim the rebate and re-entered secretly. A veritable merry-go-round of animals and vegetables is possible.

Of course, the situation is not insoluble. Something similar exists today with agricultural exports bearing subsidies between Britain and Ireland. But the VAT would expand the scope of the potential profits from smuggling to every agricultural export.

There are at least three ways to counter the difficulties (apart from stricter

---

[7] Council of the EEC: *Proposed Third Directive*, op.cit., Art. 5.

patrols to stop smuggling). One is to channel all exports of agricultural goods through government agencies, so that checks can be kept on the goods exported, and on the pattern of rebate claims by exporters. Any suspicious trend in such exports would come to light more readily and quickly through public sector marketing than through the private sector.

Another way out of the impasse is not to give any rebates on agricultural exports. This would either increase the price of agricultural exports (because farmers' costs have risen by the VAT on their inputs), or reduce farmers' or middlemen's profits (as they absorb the VAT). There is no point in the government avoiding paying the rebate to farmers (which creates the incentive to smuggle) by paying it instead to the importer across the border. Financial arrangements between exporters and importers could quickly split the profits of successful smuggling.

There is no easy way out of this difficulty. The final possible solution would be to free major farm inputs from VAT (say, by zero rating) thereby freeing the farmer of this burden. But this is completely against the decision of the EEC to extend the VAT to agriculture. However, as long as a country is not a member of the EEC and yet adopts the VAT, the most sensible solution to the problem of agricultural exports (and incidentally to the whole VAT structure in agriculture) is to exempt fertilizers, seeds, and farm machinery from VAT. To avoid punching large holes in the VAT structure, it might be better for the government to pay the farmer a rebate on the VAT content of these inputs. Then the farmer is free of tax, and the abuse of the export rebate would be avoided. Foodstuffs would not be liable to VAT. Food sold domestically could bear a special retail sales tax, which could be equivalent to the VAT it would have borne had the farmer been included in the scheme.

Once Britain or any other country is a full member of the EEC then the comprehensive VAT on agriculture with a common tax rate would remove these problems as no rebate is made on agricultural exports.

Agricultural retail sales

If a farmer can sell his output directly to the public, this forms a transaction which is extremely difficult to check. As the farmer does not pay VAT directly, and as the purchaser in this case is not a registered person (as, for instance, a cattle dealer or vegetable wholesaler would be), there need be no record of the sale. In this way, a farmer could circumvent the entire VAT liability of the distribution chain. The higher the rate of VAT, the greater the temptation because the rewards from evasion rise in direct proportion to the rate of tax. At low rates of VAT, it is not worth the inconvenience. At high rates, it most certainly is.

Farmers are always tempted to sell some produce direct to the public, e.g., milk, eggs, vegetables, thereby avoiding income and sales taxes. Many countries accept such a loss. But with high VAT rates, in countries with large farming communities, the normal retail outlets could justifiably feel discriminated against. It is difficult to see any way round this problem except to enact legislation which gives the authorities the power to curb blatent examples of direct sales by farmers to the public.

An alternative might be to tax farm inputs under the VAT at some rate *higher* than normal, but not tax farmers by any other sales tax on farm output. Thus the high rate of VAT on farm inputs would include the usual VAT and, in addition, an amount approximately equal to the VAT foregone on stages after the farm input. It would then be immaterial whether farm output was sold through normal channels or direct to the public, or indeed whether it was exported or not. Such a policy would probably have to be agreed between all members of a customs union.

Summary

    (a) The VAT should be extended to agriculture, otherwise either the farmer will be taxed unfairly, or a cascade will be introduced into the farm system.

    (b) Farmers can be treated either as normal producers under the VAT, or use a 'global credit offset' which is claimed by the purchaser of farm output as a credit against his tax liability.

    (c) The official EEC directive on the taxation of agricultural output confuses an already confusing situation; but the computation can be simplified.

    (d) If the credit offset is fixed at a rate which precisely offsets the VAT content of farm inputs, the system is neutral.

    (e) In practice, such an ideal situation is most unlikely.

    (f) The credit offset, if put at a high rate, could subsidize farming; if set at a low rate, it could penalize farming.

    (g) Such a low rate for the credit offset might encourage farmers to become full members of the VAT structure and this could improve farm bookkeeping, and increase information on farm income and expenditure.

    (h) A common reduced rate of VAT for agriculture (about 7%) is proposed for the EEC. Zero rating is probably the best solution to *exempt* food.

    (i) Great difficulties are possible in administering a VAT rebate on exports of agricultural goods if Britain or any country is not within the EEC yet adopts a VAT.

    (j) Because credit offsets on exports of agricultural goods could be claimed, large profits could be made from smuggling.

    (k) The peculiarities of farm output, with numerous individual sellers, many unidentifiable products, and relatively easy communications across land borders, increase the difficulties of administering the VAT on agricultural goods.

    (l) One way to check some of these difficulties is to channel agricultural exports through government agencies or to require farmers who export to be fully registered members of the VAT structure.

(m) Another way to avoid some of the difficulties is to give no rebates on agricultural exports.

(n) It might be possible to relieve farm purchases of fertilizers, seeds, and machinery from VAT and to impose an equivalent retail sales tax on food.

(o) A further difficulty of a high rate sales tax on agriculture is the incentive this creates for direct sales by farmers to the public.

5. The choice of rates

Progression and rates of tax

The EEC directive refers to a normal rate[1] but also allows for rates below and/or above the normal rate. No indication is given as to which classes of goods should be favoured or penalized. The only proviso is that where a transport service has a rate other than the normal, all means of transport (except private cars) should be treated equally.

On the other hand, there is a strong wish to soften the introduction of sales taxation by trying to reduce the regressiveness inherent in the tax. The usual way to do this is to levy lower rates on items which form a large part of lower income household budgets, and higher rates on those items which are bought only by the better off (or feckless) households. Only Belgium and France levy the luxury rate and it is these two countries that also attempt to operate a four-rate system.

There are three problems here. First, the more 'progressive' the sales tax is made by rate and product differentiation, the less revenue is likely to be obtained. If a truly low rate is levied on the broad categories of goods bought by large numbers of poorer households, the yield will be small and the tax regressive. Likewise, the trinkets and pleasures of the rich will, even if heavily taxed, not yield substantial revenue; quite apart from the possibility that the better off members of society might shift their consumption pattern to those goods taxed at lower rates. If high tax rates are used, goods could prove to have a high price elasticity, so that the volume bought would drop as the tax was imposed; thus the tax yield would be lower.

On a long run basis, as household incomes rise and consumption patterns extend to more of the expensive consumer durables, the tax yield will increase, but so will the regressiveness of the tax.

This is especially so when the second difficulty is considered. The goods which form a much greater proportion of low income household expenditure (tobacco and alcohol particularly) are precisely those which tend to be taxed

---

[1] Council of the EEC: Second Directive, 'On the Form and Methods of Application of the Common System of Taxation on Value-Added', *Journal Officiel des Communautes Europeenes*, No. 71, Brussels, 14 April 1967.

at higher rates. If it was genuinely desired to increase the progressiveness of sales taxation, the lowest rates of all would be applied to food, tobacco, alcohol, and TV sets. High rates would be applied to private transport, and services such as hotels, restaurants, golf clubs, hairdressers, etc. In fact, alcohol and tobacco taxation increase the regressiveness of our present tax system and it is difficult to imagine legislation for new taxes lightening that load. It is awkward to construct an acceptable rate differentiation which would significantly increase the progressiveness of the VAT.

Table 5.1
Effective rates of VAT (1 January 1971)

	Rates %			
	Lowest	Intermediate	Normal	Luxury
EEC				
Luxembourg	4		8	
Belgium (proposed)	6	14	18	25
*France	7·53	17·65	23·45	33·33
Germany	5·5		11	
Italy (proposed) (a)			10	
(b)	6		12	18
Netherlands	0	4	14	
Others				
Denmark			15	
Norway			20	
*Sweden			17·65	
*Finland			12·4	
Ireland (proposed)	5·26		16·37	30·26

* The rates shown are the *effective* rates of tax, but in France the nominal (published) rates are 19%, 7%, 15%, and 25%, in Sweden it is 15%, and in Finland 11%.

The great bulk of sales taxes redistributes not vertically with regard to income, but horizontally.[2] Thus, those in one income bracket who smoke and drink subsidize those in roughly the same income bracket who do not; those who drive cars subsidize those who travel by bus, and so on. The progressive character of indirect taxation is imparted mainly by taxes on private motoring and rates. British indirect taxation is, as a whole, regressive. The highly regressive character of sales taxes on beer and tobacco is ameliorated by taxes on motoring, expensive consumer durables, and wines and spirits.

If a highly selective VAT, levied at multiple rates, is to yield a revenue equal to the present sales taxes, the rates of tax on some of the selected items would have to be high. Alternatively, if low rates are applied to a broad

[2] Peacock, A. T: *Income Re-Distribution and Social Policy*, Cape, London, 1954.

range of goods, the result is likely to be regressive. To produce progressiveness, the combination needed is a single-tax rate which will yield a revenue equivalent to the existing sales taxes; this revenue can then be used for transfers to lower income groups.

An attractive advantage to this system is that the sales tax then ceases to influence consumer choice. With the same tax applying across the board, the consumer makes his choice between equally taxed articles. Household income may be augmented by transfer payments and from this increase more goods can be bought. But the spending of the income on different sorts of goods is not biased by the tax. Saving (untaxed) may be made more attractive. This sort of solution should be more attractive to the liberal viewpoint in that the individual is ensured social equity through the transfers, but at the same time the market determines the allocation of goods and services.

Of course, it can be held that the British purchase tax was designed not to be neutral. It has been used deliberately as a regulator to damp down, and then encourage, demand in selected sectors. But this demand control aspect of sales taxes has been criticized. It crudely alters the basis on which management makes investment decisions. It may, therefore, crucially affect future growth in those very industries where bottlenecks occur. It also implies selectivity which may make invidious distinctions between those industries selected to be penalized and those not.

Another disadvantage of using a single-rate VAT combined with substantial transfer payments to low income households, is that differential sales tax rates can also reflect social priorities. The main reason why Continental VAT rates are higher than a replacement VAT for purchase tax and SET in Britain (which would need to be about 6%) is that Britain relies more heavily on excise duties than do Continental countries. The distinction between excises, customs, and turnover taxes is partly semantic as all are taxes on sales, but Britain evolved a tax structure which gave excises a prominent role. Thus the tax system looks quite different to those on the Continent.

Thus, countries in the EEC can afford to have high VAT rates if, at the same time, their excises are low. Britain's high excises make Continental VAT rates look impossibly high to apply domestically. Before a VAT at rates comparable to those on the Continent could be applied in Britain, a redefinition of the British tax base would be needed, switching some of the tax revenue from excises to the new VAT. For instance, if all excises on drink, tobacco, and oil, and purchase tax and SET were to be replaced by VAT, the rate of VAT would need to be about 20%.

But this is not as simple as it sounds at first. The reason excises are used is first, for revenue (which could equally well come from the VAT) and second, to discriminate deliberately against expenditures that are considered luxury and/or 'morally undesirable'. This judgement reflects the patterns of social values, in that it taxes heavily alcoholic drink, tobacco, and motoring.

It is interesting that the total proportion of taxes on expenditure in Britain (47·5%) is close to other European countries. The comparable proportion for Belgium is 49·5%, Germany 40·7%, France 45·9%, and Denmark 47·4%. Despite this broad similarity, there is a marked divergence in composition. In other countries, general turnover taxes (like the VAT) account for between 38% and 19% of total tax revenue. In Britain, there is no comparable general tax, but the purchase tax (which could be compared to the French VAT at four rates) yields only 7·5% of total tax revenue. When expressed as a percentage of total taxes on expenditure, the difference is even more pronounced. The Continental countries vary between 67% and 54%, while Britain obtains only some 15% of her total taxes on expenditure from the wide based purchase tax.

Table 5.2
British and Continental sales tax structures

Country	Taxes as a percentage of total taxation, 1966			
	All sales taxes	General sales taxes	Excises	Employers contribution to social security
France	34	24	11	27
Germany	29	18	11	15
Belgium	37	25	12	21
Netherlands	25	13	12	—
Italy	33	17	16	—
Denmark	43	18	25	2
Norway	40	28	11	11
Sweden	32	15	17	9
UK	35	11	24	7
Ireland	50	8	43	3

Source: OECD Statistics of National Accounts

On the other hand, her reliance on special taxes on spirits, beer, and tobacco is most marked. In terms of the proportion of total tax revenue, Britain relies three times as heavily as the nearest EEC tax authority (Germany) on taxing alcoholic drink, four times more heavily on taxing beer than France, and five times more heavily on taxing tobacco than France (and indeed, almost nine times more so than the US).

The criticism can be made that these comparisons reflect consumption pattern differences rather than tax differences, i.e., if Britain has three times as much revenue from tax on spirits, this could merely reflect three times more consumption at the same rate. But when tax *rates* are compared, a similar pattern emerges. (See Table 8.1.)

If Britain were to match the EEC movement towards the higher rates of VAT and the eventual harmonization at some rate near 15% to 20%, a corollary might be a reduction in excises of over half on spirits, 75% on beer, and about 50% on tobacco. Of course, the VAT would be imposed on these items and increase their price again, but this would almost certainly leave them significantly cheaper than they are now. This image of a more Continental Britain might be called 'the British Continental package'.

It does, of course, involve the shift of taxation away from those 'morally' less defensible items of consumption to the broad range of consumer final demand. This could well prove unpopular with certain sections of the community. On the other hand, such a shift in taxation would not be as regressive as an across-the-board increase in sales taxes without any offsetting excise reductions, since low income families devote substantial parts of their household budgets to alcohol and tobacco consumption. Moreover, one of the aims of the EEC is to harmonize its excise duties, so if Britain becomes a member, she will have to swallow some of her value judgements on 'moral' taxes and move towards the structure accepted by the EEC. For instance, the proposed *ad valorem* excise rate for the Community for cigarettes would be 40% (compared to 77% for Britain at the moment).[3]

It should be noted that if the Community maintains the dual structure of the VAT and excises, then theoretically the two are quite separate taxes. The VAT can be levied at a single uniform rate, and the excises can be imposed at a separate non-deductable stage.

The third problem about multiple VAT rates is that different rates of VAT tend to destroy the tax as a tax on value added at some stages. This is dealt with on page 15 under the heading 'Catching up'.

There is one powerful argument in favour of different VAT rates, at least to start with. The introduction of the VAT nearly always means a broadening of the tax base, taxing some items which were hitherto untaxed. To soften the transition, low rates can be used for those items which traditionally are associated with high expenditure in low income families (food and fuel). But it should be clearly stated that this is not really introducing much progressiveness into the VAT structure. Basically, if progressiveness is wanted, then it should be obtained by income taxation and transfers. The VAT is not designed to create progressiveness and in fact will not be used to do so because it would mean low taxation of items which have a bad 'moral' tone, e.g., tobacco.

The important thing to keep in mind is the *overall* progressiveness of the tax system, mainly created by income taxes and transfers. Of course, even transfers may have difficulty in creating progressiveness. The relative position of households after allowing for both sales tax increases and increased transfers can emphasize the difficulty of adequately compensating the lower/

[3] Dosser, D. and Han S. S: *Taxes in the E.E.C. and Britain: The Problems of Harmonisation*, PEP, London, 1968, p. 28.

middle income range family, where the income is primarily earned. In this case, the family's tax liability is negligible while its only claim might be the child allowance, hence many transfer increases do not benefit it at all, yet it has to pay the increased sales taxes.

If a VAT is to be introduced, it is more efficient to have a single rate to yield a high revenue and to use that revenue to redistribute income to lower and needy groups. It is more efficient because:

(a) The administration of a single-rate VAT is much easier and cheaper than that of a multi-rate VAT.

(b) A single-rate VAT creates no possibility of inequities between producers, whereas the multiple rate does.

(c) Any 'progression' which occurs because of multiple rates does so because of consumption patterns; this in no way allows for equal treatment of those in like circumstances.

(d) The relative prices of goods and services are distorted and hence consumer choice is crudely influenced by government intervention. The allocation of resources is altered in an unpredictable way.

(e) Progression through differential rates relies on a low price elasticity of demand. If elasticity is high then a small proportion of the tax may be passed on and it ceases to be progressive according (even remotely) to income and becomes a tax on businesses. If this happens, as noted in chapter 1, it is more sensible to consider a different form of VAT, i.e., by direct assessment on wages and profits. (It should be noted that multiple rates combined with direct assessment can create problems for a multi-product firm. The necessary requirement would be that inputs attributable to one output would have to be deducted from that output if they were to be liable to a special rate of tax. This means that all inputs would have to be allocated to a particular output, and this could prove difficult, if not impossible, in many multi-product firms.)

(f) The single rate could yield a high revenue which would allow substantial payments to low income groups on the basis of *need*, not consumption. Government policy will, thereby, be based on certainty rather than uncertainty.

(g) Multiple rates give the taxpayer the opportunity to evade the tax by a misclassification of goods. As one of the main administrative arguments in favour of the VAT is that it is a check to tax evasion, it seems inconsistent to create possible loopholes.

Option to multiple rates

Multiple rates suffer from the disadvantages outlined above. It is possible to adjust the yield of the tax by altering the base on which a single rate is applied rather than altering the rate. For instance, a rate of 10% applied to a base of 100 yields £10. If the rate is left at 10% but the base is halved to 50, the yield falls to £5. In this way, the rate structure can remain unaltered, but the tax liability can be changed. In Sweden, this is the method adopted to lower the rate of VAT on buildings. The tax base for buildings is reduced to 60% of the market price, and similarly the base for services, for example, water supplies, roads, bridges, harbours, etc., is reduced to 20% of normal. France uses the same system to reduce the tax impact on books (70% of the market price) and land (33·33% of the market price).

Another way to reduce the tax liability, while leaving the rate unchanged, simply is to refund the tax. This is done on houses in Denmark. Here there is a flat-rate refund, calculated at a set rate per square metre of floor area and this is, in effect, a total refund of the VAT charged on a typical dwelling house.

Catching up

The preference for a single rate is enhanced when the difficulty of taxing actual value added is considered. Table 2.3 showed how two rates (example B) or three rates (example C) could involve a taxpayer at one stage in a liability higher than that which he ought to bear if his actual value added were used as the tax base. This arises because the EEC uses the indirect method. If the direct method were used, $t(O - I)$, then only the value added would be taxed, but it would mean that the tax content of a commodity could not be known from its selling price, because the tax liability would depend on the different rates of tax on the various inputs. (Two identical goods could have different tax contents if the producers had different input ratios.)

If the EEC method is accepted (and it is sensible to know what the tax liability is, since this is important at frontiers where goods are exported or imported), then there is the problem of varying tax liability. This can also work in reverse. If the rates on the previous stage were higher than the stage in the example, then the net credit claim against the state would be left.

Example B in Table 5.3 is reproduced from Table 2.3 showing how the tax liability of the taxpayer at this stage, paying a rate of 20% on his selling price, is increased because the credit he can claim against his tax liability is limited to £25 as the energy input is taxed at the low rate of 5%. In this case, the state 'catches up' and collects its full tax, penalizing the taxpayer at this stage. It should be noted that the taxpayer is only 'penalizied' if he in fact pays the tax. If he passes the tax on fully, then there is no tax liability actually paid by the taxpayer at this stage. Eventually, the total tax will be paid by the final consumer. It is only if the taxpayer at each stage absorbs some of the tax that there is a penalty involved.

In example D, the position is reversed. The inputs have higher tax rates (20%) than the output (5%). Thus the credit the taxpayer can claim under the indirect subtractive method of assessing tax liability (line c), is £40; but his total liability is only £15. Logically, this means he has a tax liability of £−25;

i.e., a claim against the state for £25. The EEC Commission recognized the problems involved in negative 'catching up' and dealt rather summarily with the difficulty outlined in D, but not with that in B. The reason for the rather simple approach of the Commission is the assumption underlying all EEC directives that the tax will be passed forward fully. This deals with example B. If tax credits are higher than tax liabilities, example D, the rate structure must be altered. 'Each reduced rate is to be fixed in such a manner that the amount of the tax on value added resulting from the application of

Table 5.3

VAT and 'catching up'

	B				D			
	Price exclu-sive of tax £	Tax rate %	Tax paid £	Price inclu-sive £	Price exclu-sive of tax £	Tax rate %	Tax paid £	Price inclu-sive £
Inputs:								
Raw materials	100	20	20	120	100	20	20	120
Energy	100	5	5	105	100	20	20	120
	200			225	200			240
Value added:								
Wages and profits	100		35	135	100		−25	75
Output	300	20	60	360	300	5	15	315

(a) t(W + P); 0·2 (100) = 20   0·2 (100) = 20
(b) t(O − I); 0.2 (300–200) = 20   0·2 (300–200) = 20
(c) tO − tI; 0·2 (300) − 0·05 (100) − 0·2 (100)   0·05 (300) −; ·2 (200) =
     = 60 − 5 − 20 = 35   15 − 40 = −25

this rate will normally permit the deduction of the entire tax on value added.'[4] This means no rate must be so low as to result in a tax credit large enough to offset more than the tax liability.

Although easy to write, this may not be so straightforward in practice. The size of the tax liability depends on the size of the value added. If, in an extreme case, value added were zero then it is quite possible to concoct a case where the credit becomes larger than the liability without changing the tax rates but allowing the value added to change, as shown in Table 5.4.

[4] Council of the EEC: *Second Directive*, op.cit., Article 9 (2).

Example E is much the same as example D in Table 5.3, except that the lower rate instead of being 5% is now 15%. This now gives a tax liability sufficiently large to yield a positive result after deducting tax credit on the inputs (£45 − £40). However, by keeping exactly the same tax rates, but allowing the value added to drop to zero, example F shows how the total tax liability on output is not £30, but the tax credit on sales is £40. This leaves the businessman with a net claim of £10 on the state. Ironically, this is a case where by doing *nothing* (zero value added), the businessman creates a claim on the state. (This could be the situation where a nationalized industry

Table 5.4

Further examples of VAT and 'catching up'

	E				F			
	Price exclusive of tax £	Tax rate %	Tax paid £	Price inclusive of tax £	Price exclusive of tax £	Tax rate %	Tax paid £	Price inclusive of tax £
Inputs:								
Raw materials	100	20	20	120	100	20	20	120
Energy	100	20	20	120	100	20	20	120
Value added:								
Wages and profits	100		5	105	0		−10	−10
Output	300	15	45	345	200	15	30	230

(a) t(W + P); 0·15 (100) = 15   0·15 (O) = 0

(b) t(O − I); 0·15 (300–200) = 15   0·15 (200–200) = O

(c) tO − tI; 0·15 (300) − 0·2 (200) = 45 − 40 = 5   0·15 (200) − 0.2 (200) = 30 − 40 = −10

selling a good liable to a low rate of tax made a loss and the VAT on output was smaller than the tax liability on inputs.)

So the bald statement that 'reduced rates be fixed in such a manner that the amount of VAT resulting from the application of a reduced rate will *normally* permit a credit for the entire VAT previously paid'[5] (author's italics) is not good enough. It is not merely the rates, but the amount of value added as well, which are variable, and the amount of value added is not

[5] International Bureau of Fiscal Documentation: *European Taxation: The Common System of Tax on Value Added*, Vol. 7, Nos. 7/8, Amsterdam, July/August 1967, p. 187.

within the control of the state. 'Member States will have to determine care-fully average profit margins in the particular lines of business involved.'[6]

This unsatisfactory state of affairs in the reduced rate case worsens when we look at the increased rate case. The official line here is: 'Similar rules with respect to the level at which increased rates are to be set are not provided in the Directive. As increased rates are expected to apply only to luxury goods and then only in the final taxable stage, a similar problem does not arise.'[7] This is imprecise. It is true only if it is assumed that the tax is passed

Table 5.5
Multiple rates and 'catching up'

	B				G			
	Price exclu-sive of tax £	Tax rate %	Tax paid £	Price inclu-sive of tax £	Price exclu-sive of tax £	Tax rate %	Tax paid £	Price inclu-sive of tax £
Inputs:								
Raw materials	100	20	20	120	40	20	8	48
Fuel	100	5	5	105	160	5	8	168
	200		25	225	200		16	216
Value added:								
Wages and profits	100		35	135	100		44	144
Output	300	20	60	360	300	20	60	360

(a) t(W + P); 0·2 (100) = 20   0·2 (100) = 20
(b) t(O − I); 0·2 (300−200) = 20   0·2 (300−200) = 20
(c) tO − tI; 0·2 (300) − 0·2 (100) − 0·05 (100) =   0·2 (300) − 0·2 (40) − 0·05
    60 − 25 = 35   (160) =60 − 16 = 44

forward fully. Also, admittedly, rates higher than normal are only expected to apply to luxury goods, but some rates *lower* than normal, e.g., fuel, buildings, and installations[8] in France, could apply as an input to a product which itself was to be taxed at a higher rate. Moreover, though cars might be considered a luxury, they are certainly a very widespread one, and so the problem becomes more general.

[6] Ibid., p. 188.
[7] Ibid., p. 187, footnote 288.
[8] Forte, F: 'On the Feasibility of a Truly General Value Added Tax: Some Reflections on the French Experience', *National Tax Journal*, December 1966, p. 343.

In France, where four tax rates are used, it is possible for a low rate (say, on fuel at 17·65%), to be followed by a high rate, e.g., the normal rate of 23·45%, where fuel is an input.

Example B was explained in Table 5.3. The taxpayer has a liability different to that which a true application of value added would yield (£35 instead of £20). Example G is the same position, but the ratio of inputs is changed (assuming either more efficient buying of raw materials and less efficient purchase of fuel for the same quantities as B, or using technology in such a way that raw materials are used more economically and replaced by higher fuel usage). Although in G, by better buying or more efficient production

Table 5.6
Absorbing VAT and 'catching up'

	H				I			
	Price exclusive of tax £	Rate %	Tax £	Price inclusive of tax £	Price exclusive of tax £	Rate %	Tax £	Price inclusive of tax £
Inputs:								
Raw materials	100	20	20	120	100	20	20	120
Fuel	90	5	4.5	94.5	100	5	5	105
	100		24.5	214.5	200		25	225
Value added:								
Wages and profits	100		33.5	133.5	90		33	123
Output	290	20	58	348	290	20	58	348

methods, the producer lowers his input bill to £216 tax inclusive, he gets no advantage from this, because his tax bill is automatically increased through the 'catching-up' mechanism by £9 over that of the producer in B, so that their two selling prices are the same at £360. The tax differential gives no incentive towards efficient resource use and, therefore, no substitution effect.

Up to the moment, the two producers are no worse or better off because their value added, *net of tax*, at £100 remains the same. But if one manufacturer *decided to pay part of his tax liability out of his value added* to compete against other producers, then tax is, in effect, falling on wages and profits. There is now a double differential tax problem. First, there is the possibility of profitable substitution between factors in the same firm and second, different efficiencies between two firms. In example B raw materials are taxed at 20%, fuel at 5%, wages at 35%, and profits at 35%. This will tend to discriminate against wages. If there is an alternative (see Table 5.6) between an equal percentage reduction in fuel, or in labour, then the reduction in wages will leave the company with a smaller tax bill (£33) than would the equal reduction in fuel (£33·5) if the firm decides to sell £10 cheaper, and makes a saving on fuel and on wages.

Thus, when the VAT is paid out of wages and profits, the differential rates can encourage substitution of one factor for another. As wages in the example are taxed at the normal rate, any differential rate lower than the normal will encourage substitution of that product for labour. (See also chapters 6 and 7.)

When the VAT is paid out of wages and profits and not passed on fully, those companies who can substitute a factor taxed at a lower rate for one taxed at a higher rate will gain an advantage. As labour (wages) would appear the most obvious candidate for such substitution, this effect could be claimed as an advantage in countries like Britain or Germany where labour shortages often create supply bottlenecks. But such an effect might well work in direct opposition to, for instance, the SET.

When the Continental taxes on value added are considered in this light, it is clear that some care has been taken to avoid these substitution effects. Clearly the substitutions can only take place where factors are substitutable. If, for example, raw materials and fuel are taxed at differential rates, there is usually no way to substitute, e.g., a bigger fuel input for a smaller raw material input, to obtain the same output. There may be dried foods or rubber substitutes which could be produced either by a long fuel consuming process or by a shorter process using less fuel and more raw materials, but such cases are rare. Therefore, one of the conditions for multiple rates is to apply them to commodities which are in quite separate vertical commodity flows, e.g., food, passenger transport, and so on.

But this still leaves the case of the firm which decides not to pass the tax on fully. It would be a considerable invasion of a firm's privacy to oblige it to pass on tax fully, even if it were possible to check whether it did so. After all, the tax is levied after the firm has decided the selling price and who is to say that part of the tax had not been anticipated and value added adjusted accordingly? Therefore, in this position, it is possible that wages would be discriminated against if any input was taxed at a lower rate than the firms output.

Different rates at the final stage

Up to the moment, only different rates at stages before the last have been discussed. In all cases, the application of differential rates has not altered the price to, or the tax burden on, the final consumer. It is clear that a reduced rate levied at the retail level would reduce the consumer's tax liability, e.g., if £240 worth of goods with a VAT content of £40, i.e., 20%, are bought by a retailer and he adds £40 of value making the total tax exclusive value

£240, if the retail sale is then taxed at 15%, then the tax liability is £46 — £40 = £6, and the consumer pays only 15% and not 20% (see Table 5.7). The reverse is true of a higher rate at the final stage.

Table 5.7
A retail sale taxed at 15%, but the standard rate at 20%

	Price exclusive of tax £	Tax rate %	Tax paid £	Price inclusive of tax £
Inputs	200	20	40	240
Value added	40			
Output	240	15	46	286

The cynic might remark that in the position where the consumer is to have a higher or lower rate imposed at the retail level and where the VAT is passed forward, then the whole effect of the tax could much more easily be achieved by a straightforward retail sales tax. The revenue would be the same, the effect the same, and the administration cheaper. Of course, there are other arguments in favour of the VAT. (See chapters 6, 7, and 9.)

Harmonized rates

The intention of the EEC is to have the same rates of VAT applied to the same ranges of goods throughout the Community. During 1970, the Commission proposed to the EEC Council that a timetable be arranged to achieve substantial harmonization of VAT rates by 1975. By this time, it was proposed that only two rates should operate. A standard rate varying between limits of 12% and 18%, and a lower rate varying between limits of 5·5% and 7·5%.

By 1978, the differences in the standard rate were forecast to be reduced to only 3% (as opposed to 6% above). Thereafter, complete harmonization would be achieved. The final step would be the conversion of the entire VAT system to an origin principle for trade within the Community (retaining the destination principle for trade with countries outside the EEC).

Whether this timetable can be implemented is doubtful. Already, the introduction of the VAT is two years behind schedule; Italy has not yet introduced it. Countries have experienced considerable public dissension over the general changes in prices due to the introduction of the new tax. (See chapter 10.) Changes in relative prices would be equally unsettling, particularly for countries like Belgium and France where the luxury rate would have to be abandoned, and this implies a reduction from the present maximum rate of 33·33% in France to about 15%. As mentioned earlier, such substantial variations in relative prices imply very fundamental changes in the relative values placed both publicly and privately on goods.

One way out of this difficulty might be to allow countries to operate a flexible base for a limited number of goods. So that, for instance, a car might be liable to the standard rate of VAT at 15%, but this could be adjusted by specifying the base to be 200%, so that the effective rate of tax becomes 30%.

Revenue

Whatever rates are chosen, one of the most attractive aspects of the VAT is the large and buoyant revenue it can produce. Second, the introduction of the VAT gives governments the opportunity to recast, not only their sales taxes, but also the structure of their transfer payments.

The buoyancy of the tax is easily appreciated as it covers all sales. If the tax is truly general, no matter which part of the economy is expanding, the VAT will respond at once to that activity. (This has implications for the VAT as a built-in stabilizer, a point which is discussed in chapter 9.) As it is sensible to subsume most sales taxes under the VAT, it usually assumes a prominent position in total government revenue. France relies most on the VAT and collects 40% of her tax revenue from it. Germany gets about 25% of her tax revenue from the VAT, Denmark and Holland 20%.

The introduction of the VAT is a substantial tax reform in any country. The upheaval can be used to sort out other parts of the tax structure at the same time. If a simple single or double rate VAT is used, then the government will feel obliged to offset some of the likely regressive nature of the new tax by substantial transfer payments to lower income households. This, in turn, gives the government some flexibility in altering social transfer payments. Only Denmark took the opportunity created by introducing the new tax to overhaul her whole tax structure. Other countries have tried to win public support for the new tax by promising that it is only a tax substitution and does not involve a net increase in sales tax revenue.

Summary

(a) Differential rates are used to try to reduce the regressiveness of a high rate sales tax.

(b) It is probably misguided to use differential rates for progressiveness, as to do so would require a substantial reduction in the taxation of tobacco and alcohol, as well as food.

(c) It is more efficient to levy a single rate and use the excess revenue for transfers to low income households. Administration is easier, inequity reduced, and progression ensured.

(d) Multiple rates can be avoided by alterations in the tax base, by refunds or by excises.

(e) The indirect subtractive method with multiple rates causes tax liabilities to diverge from actual value added.

(f) The EEC has dealt with the extreme case of tax claims against the state, but not in an entirely satisfactory manner.

(g) If firms absorb part of the VAT liability, and multiple rates are used, there is the possibility of discrimination against certain factors, particularly wages.

(h) The effect of lower or higher rates at the final stage could be obtained more efficiently using a single-stage retail sales tax.

(i) It is proposed to harmonize rates of VAT throughout the Community so that by 1975 the standard rate should lie between 12% and 18%, and the lower rate between 5·5% and 7·5%

(j) Difficult changes in relative prices might be met by a flexible attitude to altering tax bases rather than tax rates.

(k) If the VAT rate forms a substantial part of total tax revenue, it yields great tax buoyancy, and can allow flexibility in transfer payments.

6. The VAT replacing sales taxes: effects on prices, income distribution, investment, efficiency, and the balance of payments

Everyone wants to know what will be the effects of a new tax like the VAT. The effects on prices are usually uppermost in the public's mind, but businessmen ask about exports and investment, and the government is interested in encouraging efficiency and in the distributional impact. The effects will be different depending upon the taxes that the VAT replaces or supplements. There are infinite permutations on tax substitution, but we must narrow the field of discussion.

First, it can be assumed that the VAT replaces sales taxes only, or second, that it replaces some other tax or taxes on businesses. So many important issues are raised by the possibility of altering company taxation and employers' contributions to social security payments that a limited discussion of this option is included in chapter 7. Finally, in chapter 8, the possibility of the VAT replacing excises, the SET, and income tax is discussed.

The effects of the VAT replacing sales taxes are, for the purposes of this chapter, divided into five interrelated parts:

- (a) Prices.
- (b) Income distribution.
- (c) Investment.
- (d) Efficiency.
- (e) Balance of payments.

As stressed already, the basic distinction to be grasped in discussing the effects of the VAT is whether it is passed on fully, or absorbed. If passed on fully, it is a sales tax. If absorbed, it is a tax on wages and profits. This is particularly important when the effects of the VAT on companies are considered. Some discussion of current economic opinion on this issue of sales tax shifting will indicate the difficulties involved, but will also help to pin down the likely patterns of shifting under the introduction of a VAT.

Shifting and consumption taxes

The first point to be made is that shifting in a macro-economic sense can become so diffuse as to be almost meaningless. Suppose commodity prices rise following a sales tax imposition. If capital goods are not taxed (as under the VAT) then the prices of final goods have risen relative to capital goods. 'Relative positions with regard to present earnings are unchanged—, but relative positions in terms of future earnings are improved for the saver'.[1] On the other hand, if the prices of consumer goods rise and consumer incomes rise sufficiently to maintain their previous real consumption, then the shifting of the tax starts to depend on things like the unused resources in the economy, the money supply, trade union power, etc.

In general, it is almost impossible to isolate the effects of a given tax change. In the theoretical world, so many other variables must be taken into account, e.g., the use to which government revenue is put,[2] the degree of money illusion, other relative price changes, and government monetary policy. In the real world, there are even more complications as economic policy rarely acts in single steps. At any given moment, combined with a tax change in Britain, there could be, for example, a rise in import prices due to policy decisions outside the state, e.g., an export tax in Malaysia, a fall in gas prices due to the increased use of natural gas, a wage round which raises labour incomes, an across-the-board tariff cut under a GATT agreement, and a fall in beef prices because of oversupply from Ireland. All these are quite plausible and all would so complicate relative prices that to single out the effects of the domestic tax change alone would be difficult, if not impossible.

The general consensus of academic opinion is that consumption taxes are passed forward in part. The method adopted in this chapter is to itemize the various factors which might affect the shifting of the tax and to discuss their importance for the VAT—particularly in Britain. There are eleven points, which could be subdivided or added to, but they are probably the most important.

(a) **The market.** If the home market has been traditionally highly protected, then the government has already given producers protection against competitive imports and guarantees them protection against government increases in domestic sales taxes. An increase in domestic prices, because the tax is passed forward fully, will not necessarily make imports more competitive (the tariff could be raised, or more likely the tariff is already high

---

[1] Musgrave, R. A: *The Theory of Public Finance*, McGraw-Hill, London, 1958, p. 380–81.

[2] Due, J. F: 'Sales Taxation and the Consumer', *The American Economic Review*, December 1963.

enough to allow some latitude for domestic price increases . . . water in the tariff), and sales *vis-à-vis* other domestic manufacturers depend on the structure of the industry. For instance, Ireland has had a highly protected market and for many years producers have been able to rely on substantial protection. The Anglo-Irish Free Trade Area is starting to erode this protected position and consumption tax increases may not be so easy to pass on as previously.

A VAT introduced and combined with freer trade might force the new tax to be absorbed. Of course, the VAT is applied to imports as well as refunded on exports; it is the reduction in protection which will affect shifting, not the VAT itself. But for all countries joining the EEC this is the most likely combination—more international competition in domestic markets and the introduction of a new tax.

(b) **Industrial structure.** The fewer producers there are, the easier it is to have collusion, or even mutual sympathetic agreement, to pass consumption taxes forward. A limited number of producers in a highly protected market are in the strongest position of all. This is a more likely position in a small country.

It could be argued that such near monopoly positions might make it difficult to pass on the tax because a monopolist's price before the tax increase was likely to be that which maximized profits. But producers under protection do not necessarily exploit their position to the full, perhaps because they feel that what the government has given, the government can remove, perhaps they fear competition from government-run companies, maybe quotas of competitive imports could be used against them, and lastly they may have always wanted to leave a little leeway for price flexibility (upwards).

In so far as greater international competition reduces domestic monopoly power, the VAT may be introduced under circumstances which encourage backward, rather than forward, shifting.

(c) **Industrial cost of production.** If firms are producing with declining cost curves, the increased tax and consequent price rise might reduce the quantity demanded and increase costs. If the VAT is seen as a sales tax replacing a sales tax, then there should be no net difference. If, as is more likely, the VAT covers a wider range of goods than the tax it replaces, then there will be a change in relative prices. Some goods taxed under purchase tax might find their relative position much more favourable than, for example, services taxed under the VAT.

In this case, the net effect of substituting the VAT for purchase tax would depend on whether firms producing services were more likely to have declining cost curves than those producing goods whose prices had fallen relative to services. When the SET was introduced, it was argued that productivity was likely to be higher in manufacturing than in services and that these industries were more likely to be producing under declining cost curves.

If this is true, then the substitution of a VAT for the purchase tax would increase the quantity of manufactured goods demanded, and with economies of large scale production, prices would fall. Services taxed at high VAT rates would suffer a fall in the quantity demanded, but because of their increasing cost curves would be able to reduce prices to compensate for the increased tax.

Overall, the tax change might be beneficial, but the effectiveness depends on the relative elasticities of demand.

(d) Elasticity of demand. The great traditional revenue consumption taxes are on goods with an inelastic demand (where the quantity demanded will not change much when the price changes), e.g., salt, petrol, tobacco. At the same time, both high and low priced goods can have inelastic demand schedules; people will go on buying bread despite a 5% consumption tax, while the few people who buy diamond necklaces will also continue buying such objects despite a 5% tax.

Services might be considered to have a more elastic demand schedule than manufactured goods, i.e., people will alter their consumption when prices change. Once more, in so far as there are relative price shifts when a VAT is introduced, any price increase in services might have a substantial effect on demand reducing it so that producers might be less willing to shift the VAT forward, maintain stable prices, and thereby retain their customers.

This relative elasticity of demand can be enhanced by the coverage of the taxes.

(e) Coverage of the taxes. It can be argued that:
- (i) general taxes will be passed forward more easily than selective ones because there are no (or few) untaxed substitutes, or
- (ii) that the coverage of the tax is immaterial, it will be passed forward as long as the consumption taxes are placed on a good with an inelastic demand schedule, or
- (iii) a general tax must cover many goods for which demand is elastic and, therefore, will tend to be absorbed in many cases, or
- (iv) systems which do not tax all goods will often exempt essentials, e.g., food, and therefore invite substitution and absorbtion.

The VAT is designed to be a very general tax, covering almost all goods and services. There will be very few non-taxed substitutes, and those there are (doctors, dentists, banking?) are unlikely to present attractive alternatives. Because it is a general tax and because all the taxpayers are aware that everyone is liable for the same tax, this may encourage a tacit agreement to shift the tax forward. But this is possible only if there is a monetary expansion sufficient to finance and sustain the increased value of transactions.[3]

[3] Rolph, E. R. and Break G: *Public Finance*, Ronald Press, New York, 1961.

(f) Monetary policy. A general increase in the price level occasioned by a tax increase (or substitution) can only occur if sufficient money is made available to finance and sustain the increased value of trade (or if there is an increase in the velocity of circulation). In theory, if the money supply is not increased, then the tax can be paid only if factor payments are reduced. In practice, such a tight control over the money supply, including credit, is rarely exercised. For instance, the British practice of overdrafts instead of term loans allows firms to take up the buffer element in their overdraft when a liquidity squeeze is applied. Moreover, with wages inflexible downwards, and the prices of many raw materials dictated by externals, the tax would reduce the reward to capital—and this takes us into considerations about long term investment and the forces determining the division between profits and wages. Many European countries have difficulty in restraining the money supply and raising taxes at the same time. Of course, if the VAT is introduced as an equal yield tax substitution and the money supply is unchanged, the problem of controlling forward shifting through the money supply should not arise except where reactions to the tax substitution are perverse and the replaced tax had been absorbed but the new tax is passed on. This is precisely the position discussed in the next chapter when a VAT replaces a profits tax.

(g) Government attitude. Closely allied to the supply of money is the general government attitude to price increases consequent on tax changes. It can be argued that a government encourages producers to pass the tax forward if it:

(i) encourages traders to indicate the amount of sales tax separate to the total bill so that the tax is seen as an amount additional to price,
(ii) levies the tax on a tax exclusive base,
(iii) relies more on single-stage retail taxes than on multi-stage cascade taxes.

On the other hand, a government policy which encourages businesses to conceal the tax element and which confuses the taxpayer can also make for forward shifting, so that if a government:

(i) conceals the tax content by *taxe occulte*, cascade, and tax inclusive bases, and
(ii) has numerous rates of tax which confuse consumers, this might also encourage forward shifting of the tax.

In Britain, it has not been the practice to show the tax element clearly as a separate amount, except in some limited cases, e.g., motor cars. Also, the British consumer is accustomed to numerous different rates of tax levied at a stage before the retail sale. This probably all makes for easier forward shifting. The substitution of a VAT would be more likely to continue the forward shifting than to cause any radical re-appraisal in either business or consumer attitudes to shifting.

(h) Government expenditure. With the revenue from a sales tax, the government might subsidize the production of some goods, e.g., bread, and in this case there would be a substitution effect. Alternatively, the government might subsidize wage payments, e.g., through social security payments, and hence reduce factor costs, and so on . . . the variations are endless. Clearly, what the government does with the revenue can have an effect on the shifting. Therefore, in the second part of this chapter when the substitution of one tax for another is discussed (differential incidence), government expenditure will usually be assumed to be unaltered.

(i) Height of the tax. It can be argued that a low rate of tax will be passed on because it is insignificant. Alternatively, it can be held to be absorbed thus avoiding any disruption of the market. The higher a tax rate, the more likely it is that part of it, at least, will be passed forward.

In general, a low rate of tax has the added complication that it creates small fractions, often smaller than the lowest coinage fraction. In this position, traders will nearly always round up. The smaller the value of the goods, the more likely this is to happen. In this way small value, frequent purchases, often essentials like soap, matches, foodstuffs, are likely to bear a tax rate substantially higher than the nominal rate, e.g., the Irish retail sales tax of $2\frac{1}{2}\%$ (until 1970 when raised to 5%) on a 5p purchase would be $0\cdot125$p, in present circumstances this is most likely to be rounded up to a penny, making it 20% tax). This sort of price increase is likely to be regressive as these types of purchases (low cost and frequent), bulk larger as a percentage of low income household purchases than they do of high income households. There can be little doubt that the turnover and wholesale taxes in Ireland have created price increases of this nature, as did low rate cascade taxes on the Continent.

(j) Directions of the tax change. In general, there is evidence that producers pass forward tax increases more readily than they do tax decreases. In so far as we are more likely to be dealing with tax increases, this tends to emphasize the full passing forward of the tax.

(k) General state of the economy. If the economy is experiencing a general increase in economic activity, then it is likely that prices will rise in any case because, for example, employers will give wage increases more readily to meet deliveries on long order books, and this allows consumption increases to be passed on more easily.

Looking back over the eleven controversial points, we might summarize them by saying that as the protected market of a country is eroded by the operation of the EEC, domestic producers will find it increasingly difficult to pass on sales taxes. In so far as sales taxes in the past have been passed on, the substitution of the VAT is unlikely to encourage any radical shift to absorb the tax. As VAT rates are likely to be high, e.g., 15% to 20%, they are likely to be passed forward, and this is almost certain if the tax change is made in a period of increasing economic activity.

In general, such empirical evidence as there is[4] tends to indicate forward shifting of taxes. 'The two hypotheses that most frequently seem to be adopted in practice are:

(a) sales taxes are usually fully shifted forwards,
(b) sales taxes are usually largely, but not entirely shifted forwards.'[5]

For the second part of this chapter we will discuss the substitution of a VAT for the purchase tax (and some excises). This means that we have to make assumptions about how the present taxes are shifted, and how the VAT might be shifted. To cover all options, we assume four cases. (See Tables 6.1 and 6.2.) The four cases are:

(a) That both the VAT and the purchase tax are passed forward fully.
(b) That both the VAT and the purchase tax are fully absorbed.
(c) That the VAT is passed forward, but the purchase tax is absorbed.
(d) That the VAT is absorbed, but the purchase tax is passed forward.

For the rest of this chapter, we discuss the various effects of an equal yield VAT replacing sales taxes.

Prices

A general, equal yield VAT which replaces a general sales tax should have no effect on prices. If companies already pass sales taxes forward fully, they are likely to continue to do so with the VAT. As both taxes are general, consumers have no option of transferring to non-taxed goods or services.

However, the proposed VAT differs in at least three ways from the existing British purchase tax. First, the VAT includes the retail stage instead of stopping at the wholesale stage. Discretion is left to each country about extending the VAT to the retail stage, but it is clearly the intention of the EEC that all countries should quickly include the retail stage. Any country introducing the VAT would be well advised to organize the new tax in such a way as to include the retail stage.

Second, the VAT extends the purchase tax backwards to include all manufacturers. This does not change their tax liability if they have been liable to purchase tax, because the fractions of VAT on each stage are equivalent to the wholesale purchase tax. But many of these manufacturers traditionally extend substantial credit to their customers. To the extent that there is a necessary once and for all expansion of company liquidity to finance a VAT liability on invoice before cash is received, then companies

---

[4] *The Richardson Report*: op.cit.
Musgrave, R. A: 'Tax Policy', *Review of Economics and Statistics*, May 1964.
[5] OECD: *Border Tax Adjustments and Tax Structures*, Paris, 1968, para. 140.

may have to raise prices slightly to cover an extension of borrowing. This would be a minor influence on prices.

These substitutions would extend the tax base. If it was an equal yield substitution, the tax rate (or rates) could be lower. On the other hand, administrative expenses would be higher. (See chapter 9.) For an equal yield net of expenses, the tax rate would still be lower with a VAT than with the purchase tax.

Although the tax base is extended, the VAT is simply a fractionated way of gathering the same yield as the purchase tax. The only differences are the larger number of taxpayers, the inclusion of the retail stage, and the higher administrative expenses. As a result, either prices are higher or factor payments lower by the increased amount of the administrative expenses (which would be minute expressed as a price change distributed over all goods).

Third, the VAT differs from the purchase tax in the coverage of the goods taxed. Clearly, services are brought into the tax net, but so are many food-stuffs, fuels, housing, books, and many household goods. Roughly half the expenditure of British consumers is not directly liable to sales taxes at present. The selective employment tax now taxes services, but the rate of this as a sales tax is lower than the lowest purchase tax rate. Overall, the substitution of a general VAT for the purchase tax would be likely to involve substantial shifts in relative prices.

For instance, in Britain the tax rates on motor cars and electrical appliances would be likely to fall, but those on restaurants, hotels, transport, etc., would rise. Of course, a multi-rate VAT might parallel the rate structure of, for example, the purchase tax. But under a VAT, it is desirable to have few rates. The fewer the rates, the more likely it is that the VAT would create changes in relative prices compared to the purchase tax. These changes in prices, in turn, might create shifts in consumption.

Let us consider the shifting alternatives.

(a) Both taxes passed forward. If an equal yield VAT is substituted for purchase tax, the Richardson Committee thought the most reasonable assumption was that both taxes would be fully passed on in higher prices: 'British businesses which pay purchase tax also consider the tax as an addition to prices. They regard themselves as tax collectors . . . they are usually able to recoup the tax by passing it forward.'[6] Any estimate of the effects of removing one tax and substituting another, of the rates required, and of the changes in general prices and relative prices, must be very approximate. Table 6.1 shows such a rough attempt. Some recent figures published by the Central Statistics Office in *Economic Trends* show the allocation of individual taxes on expenditure by type of expenditure. This allows us to make some estimate of possible changes in relative prices by indirect tax substitutions. Both purchase tax and SET are at present in some part included in the value of

[6] The Richardson Committee, op. cit., para. 105.

exports and in some items of gross domestic capital formation. Under a VAT, the purchase tax and SET so included in final prices would be presumed fully recovered by manufacturers. This means that the total yield of purchase tax from consumer expenditure, shown in column 2 of Table 6.1 as £905 million, is a net figure from the total yield of purchase tax of £1108 after deducting the purchase tax element in exports and in gross domestic capital formation. In addition, the Central Statistics Office allocates some purchase tax to intermediate expenditure and this also has to be deducted to get the net purchase tax element in consumer expenditure. (A similar calculation has to be done to get the net SET element in consumer expenditure, see chapter 8.)

When the purchase tax is replaced by a VAT, then of the present £1108 million yield, we assume that £102 million would still come from intermediate expenditure; that is, we assume that the present allocation of purchase tax to intermediate expenditure represents an absorbed element of the tax by industry and that this would continue if an equal yield substitution took place. Of course, if this assumption is not accepted, then £102 million has to be added to the required replacement yield. With the replacement of the purchase tax by the VAT, the purchase tax previously collected on exports and gross domestic capital formation is assumed to fall on the new tax; therefore £101 million previously collected in this way has to be added to the present £905 million of consumer expenditure on purchase tax which makes a total of £1006 million as the desired yield, say, £1000 million.

Table 6.1 column 4 shows the tax base A which is consumer expenditure net of purchase tax. On this tax base, it would need a single-rate VAT of 3·7% to give a yield of £1000 million. But this is unrealistic. It is unlikely that any VAT substituted for purchase tax would be imposed on top of the already existing excise duties. That is, any VAT on goods already liable to excise would be adjusted in terms of the excise, leaving the net price unchanged. Therefore, in Table 6.1, we must exclude beer, wines, spirits, and tobacco from the tax base (assuming the yield from these products remains unchanged). It is probably also reasonable to exclude, as in Germany, rent, rates, water charges, communications (not personal travel), domestic service, charities, and insurance. This will reduce the tax base to £19 043 million. The average VAT now required to give a yield of £1000 million would be just over 5%.

But there is one further exemption which it is probably reasonable to accept. There is a long tradition in Britain of cheap food, and it is unlikely that any government would have the political nerve to make food liable to the VAT; certainly, not at the introduction of the tax. If food is exempted, except 'other manufactured food', then the rate required to make an equal yield tax substitution would be 7·5%. In Table 6.1, column 6, this rate of 7·5% is shown in comparison with column 2 giving the yield of purchase tax and gives some idea of the possible relative price changes for broad commodity groupings. Food would remain unchanged in price, and there might be some slight diminution of the small purchase tax element in wine,

Table 6.1

Approximate rates and yields from VAT replacing purchase tax and SET

	1 Consumer expenditure £ million	2 Purchase tax £ million	3 SET £ million	4 1 minus 2 tax base A £ million	5 1 minus 3+2 tax base B £ million	6 VAT replacing PT at 7.5% £ million	7 VAT replacing PT at rates of 5% and 10% £ million	8 VAT replacing PT and SET at rates of 10% and 20% £ million
Food (household expenditure) cereals, meat, veg, etc. other manufactured food	5783	(65)	(31)	5718	5687	—	—	—
	194	(34)	(15)	160	145	12	8	15
Beer	1073	—	3	1073	1070	—	—	—
Wine, spirits	751	4	3	747	744	—	—	—
Tobacco	1694	—	9	1694	1685	—	—	—
Housing (rent, rates, water, and maintenance)	3590	4	15	3586	3571	—	—	—
Fuel and light	1421	—	—	1421	1421	106	71	—
Clothing and footwear	2417	174	22	2243	2221	168	112	—
Motor car and motor cycles (including secondhand)	782	150	3	632	629	47	63	126
Furniture and floor coverings	588	59	6	529	523	40	53	105
Radio, electrical and other durables	587	100	4	487	483	36	49	97

Textiles, soft furnishings	695	37	6	558	552	42	56	110
Matches, soap, cleaning materials	244	8	1	236	235	18	12	24
Books, newspapers, etc.	420	—	4	420	416	32	21	42
Chemists goods	422	87	5	335	330	25	34	66
Miscellaneous recreational goods	637	68	1	569	568	43	57	113
Other miscellaneous goods	359	85	7	274	267	21	27	53
Running costs of vehicles	1518	—	16	1518	1502	113	76	150
Travel	924	—	—	924	924	69	46	92
Communication services	284	—	—	284	284	—	—	—
Entertainment and recreational	472	14	14	458	444	34	23	44
Catering and accommodation	1477	(14)	(54)	1463	1409	107	146	280
Domestic service	149	(2)	(6)	147	141	—	—	—
Wages paid by non-profit making bodies and insurance	735	(8)	—	727	727	—	—	—
Other	1470	(9)	—	1461	1461	110	146	146
Totals	28206	905	225	27301	27076	1023	1020	1563

Source: Adapted from National Income and Expenditure 1970, Table 22, and Economic Trends, November 1970, Table 3.

spirits, and housing. Other manufacturers of food would experience a substantial fall in price (approximately by two-thirds). The price of motor cars would fall, as would furniture and floor coverings, and radio, electrical, and other durables.

The fall in the price of cars would be easily offset by the large increase in the running costs of vehicles as the VAT would be imposed on top of the present hydrocarbon oil duties. Of course, it could be argued that a balance in the hydrocarbon oil excise should be made to leave the price unchanged as in the case of alcohol, but a switch from taxes on the capital cost of vehicles, to an emphasis on the marginal running costs might be no bad thing in bringing home to motorists the more realistic cost of vehicle space and running.

This substitution would involve large increases in the tax liability of fuel and light, and also in taxes on books and newspapers along with travel. Catering and accommodation would suffer a substantial tax increase. So the general picture is one of unchanged prices for food and drink and lower prices for many consumer durables, but substantial increases in the running costs of cars, entertainment, catering, and fuel and light. To make the tax more acceptable, some juggling with fuel and light and the consumer durables would probably be desirable.

The general rate of 7·5% promptly brings out a difficulty in discussing equal yield substitution. The proposed tax rate replacing the purchase tax yield at 7·5% is much lower than the standard rate in any Continental country. As the aim is to harmonize the standard rates of VAT, it is only realistic to think of rates much higher than 7·5%.

The NEDO report did not estimate the likely change in price of this simple purchase tax substitution[7] but, using similar methods, the increase in prices might be some 1·5%. The estimates in Table 6.1 show a required yield about 10% higher than the present purchase tax on consumer expenditure (assuming that the VAT is required to recoup the purchase tax at present contained in exports and capital formation). But with the emphasis on the main constituents of the cost of living index (food, drink, and housing) remaining constant, the effect on the cost of living would be much less.

It is clear that for Britain the probable increase in prices attributable to the VAT, assuming both purchase tax and VAT are passed on, would be less of a problem than the price increase stemming from other influences. In particular, the increases in food prices, when tariff protection in the EEC replaces the present agricultural subsidies, would far outweigh the problem of price increases from sales tax substitution.

If the substitution is a high yield (say 15%) for a low yield sales tax, then there will be large price changes and the macro-economic effect will depend on what the surplus revenue is used for. If the surplus revenue is used to

[7] National Economic Development Office: *Value Added Tax*, HMSO, London, 1969, paras. 5.9 to 5.14.

alter personal income tax and transfers, the direct effect on companies is likely to be negligible, but the effect on income distribution large; if it used to alter company taxes the effect could be considerable (see chapter 7).

Another possibility is that by broadening the tax base for a general equal yield tax, lower rates of tax on some commodities under conditions of decreasing costs would benefit the consumer (eventually) through the reduced costs of production.[8] The extent of such economies is likely to be small, any reduction delayed, and the passing on of any reduction to the consumer, doubtful.

(b) Both taxes absorbed. If, for some reason, the conventional sales taxes were not passed on but absorbed, and the VAT was similarly absorbed, then the two taxes are still similar. They become taxes on the factors of production. The company can try to absorb them by:

(i) Cutting wages, in which case it becomes a payroll tax.
(ii) Cutting dividends, in which case it is a tax on investment income.
(iii) Cutting the prices to raw materials suppliers. It is only in this last case that there is a difference between the VAT and the turnover and wholesale taxes.

Under the VAT, if you try to recoup tax liability by driving down raw material prices, tax credit also drops and as the value added increases so does tax liability. Retail sales taxes can be recouped entirely by forcing down raw material prices with no change at all in profits (or wages) tax liability. So if a retail sales tax were absorbed and recouped through lower raw material prices, the substitution of the VAT might result in a discrimination against wages and profits, compared to raw materials. The absorbed VAT becomes a tax on wages and profits and is, therefore, similar to (but not the same as) a profits tax. This will be discussed more fully in the next chapter.

(c) VAT passed forward, but other sales taxes absorbed. If the VAT is passed forward fully but the conventional sales taxes are absorbed, then a tax on factors is replaced by a tax on consumers. Depending on the factors relieved of tax the returns to any of them could rise. Firms would not voluntarily increase the rewards of raw material suppliers, or indeed, labour, so that the likely result will be an increase in the return to capital. This means a fall in the real income of labour due to a general price rise, and an increase in investment income. It is likely that there would be trade union pressure for wage increases to redress the balance.

(d) VAT absorbed, but other sales taxes passed forward. The opposite possibility is the absorption of the VAT and the forward shifting of the conventional sales taxes. The removal of say, the purchase tax would reduce prices

[8] Kaldor, N: *Essays on Economic Policy*, Vol. 1, Duckworth, London, 1964, p. 290.

and the absorption of VAT would not be reflected in any increase: the returns to factors of production would be reduced. Depending on the relative factor substitution possibilities and the demand elasticities, wages might fall by more than materials, or *vice versa*. These possibilities are summarized in Table 6.2 where an increase is shown as a (+) and no change (O).

Table 6.2

VAT substituted for sales taxes

Changes in	Taxes passed forward	Taxes equally absorbed	VAT passed on, sales taxes absorbed	VAT absorbed sales taxes passed on
Prices	O/+	O	+	—
Profits	O	O/—	+	—
Wages	O	O/—	O	—
Materials	O	O/+	O	—

Which of these cases is the most likely? As argued above and in later chapters, many sales taxes are likely to be passed forward. A substitution of a VAT for these taxes would create the expectation of like treatment for the new tax. In Britain, the evidence of the Richardson Committee, and indeed of the Reddaway Committee, indicated that eventually the sales tax will be passed on, even if in the short run it is absorbed because of market conditions, i.e., retail price maintenance in the case of the SET. Therefore, the option shown in column 1 is taken as the most likely for a detailed analysis of income distribution changes.

Income distribution

Both taxes passed forward. The NEDO report on value added taxation argued that 'there is little substance in the fear that the substitution of a VAT certainly if applied at two rates and with food and certain other exemptions, would be so inequitable as to be incapable of correction by way of quite small adjustments in direct benefits such as pensions or family allowances'.[9]

This was substantially borne out by a more detailed survey. A substitution of the German VAT for purchase tax and SET (but excluding food), at rates of 5·5% and 11%, assuming both taxes passed on by 75%, resulted in the annual expenditure of an old age pensioner with an income of £6 a week, falling by £2. The change for a bachelor with over £20 a week was zero, as it was for a working couple with one child. On the other hand, substituting the French VAT (effective rates at that time of 6·38%, 14·94%,

---

[9] NEDO: op. cit., para. 5.56.

19·78%, and 25%) including food, increased the cost of living for each household by some 9% to 11%.

Within these global figures there are considerable variations in the price changes for individual items. Some allowance was also made for changes in company profits taxation, but the effect of this on prices was so small as to be swamped by the purchase tax, SET, and VAT changes. For instance, all products at present taxed under the highest purchase tax rates fell in price when the German VAT, excluding food, was substituted; then expenditure on radio, TV, and electrical appliances by a single woman worker household fell by 16%, on jewellery and travel goods by 14%. Because no adjustment was made in excises, goods, already taxed heavily by excises, which became liable to the VAT rose sharply in price. When the VAT was substituted for the purchase tax, the increase in a household's cost of living, as a proportion of its income, was higher for low income than for high income households. A straightforward substitution using the German VAT (including food, as in Germany) would increase the cost of living for an old age pensioner (income £6 a week) by 8%, for a retired couple (income £6–£10 a week) by 7·5%, for a couple with one child (income (£10–£25) by 7%, for a bachelor (income £20+) by 5%, for a couple both working (income £30+) by 4·6%, and for a professional man and wife both working and with some investment income and two children (income £50+) by 4·5%.[10]

The substitution of a 15% VAT for the existing sales taxes in Ireland would be regressive. But if excises on alcohol and tobacco were reduced at the same time, although prices still increase (by 8% to 11%), the increases bear more heavily on high income households than on low ones. A further correction to the regressive nature of the tax substitution was made by using the substantial excess revenue to increase social benefits. The result of this was to compensate low income households completely for the rise in their cost of living, leaving their net position after the tax substitution unaltered. But higher income households who can claim few allowances, yet whose cost of living has risen, find themselves in a worse position. This turns the substitution in to a progressive change rather than a regressive one.

A difficulty for any country using sales taxes lies in adequately compensating households in the low to middle income range, where income is earned and, therefore, allowances are small, and whose tax liability (because income is relatively low) is negligible.

The same problem occurs if more than one tax rate is used. In each case, using the excess revenue to increase social allowances, it is possible to introduce progressiveness in that:

(a) The absolute increase in expenditure for lower incomes is smaller.

[10] See Brown, C. V: *Impact of Tax Changes on Income Distribution*, PEP, February 1971, CSRC, *Report on VAT* (unpublished) and Tait, A. A: *The Economic Consequences of Introducing a Value Added Tax into Ireland on the EEC model, covering Industrial Production, Agricultural Production, and Services*. Paper for the Economic and Social Research Institute, April 1969.

(b) The increased cost of living as a percentage of income is lower for lower income households.

(c) The net change in savings for households is remarkably progressive according to household income, i.e., low income households found they could save more after the tax substitution.

For instance, in Table 6.1, column 7 shows a replacement of the purchase tax by the VAT with rates of 5% and 10%. Because of the differential, it is possible to put the higher tax rate of 10% on those articles which are more likely to be bought by higher income households. This results in price increases in textiles and soft furnishings, the running costs of vehicles, travel, catering, and accommodation. At the same time, food and drink remain unchanged in price, while other manufactured food falls in price as does clothing and footwear, chemist's goods, and radio, electrical, and other durables.

This rough progression, by using differential tax rates, is increased the bigger and more dramatic the differential is made. For instance, a good progression in terms of income groups was obtained using rates with a spread of 2·5% to 15%. Of course, this discriminates substantially between different goods and must have considerable effects on consumer preferences. Depending on price and income elasticities, the progressiveness of such rates could be reduced by changes in the consumption pattern of households with different incomes.

All this bears out the NEDO statement quoted above, that the VAT substitution need not be inequitable. This is not to say that the VAT is a more progressive tax than, say, purchase tax. It would be possible to create more progression using the existing sales taxes. The increases in progression achieved in the theoretical substitution were obtained by greatly increasing the yield of sales taxes and using the excess to boost certain allowances; this could equally well be done using the ordinary sales taxes.

Investment

Up to now, we have ignored the problems of investment goods (commodities which help production, but last more than a year) and stocks. There are two ways in which investment can be dealt with under the VAT. The 'income variant' allows the tax element of the annual depreciation as a VAT credit against tax liability. The 'consumption variant' allows the full tax content of the capital purchase as a tax credit. Clearly, under the income variant, net capital (total expenditure less depreciation) is taxed annually. This is undesirable if an economy wishes to encourage growth. Therefore, the EEC chose the consumption variant and this would be the sensible choice for any other country adopting the VAT.

It should be noted that the consumption variant can allow a company to have a net claim against the state. If a firm buys a very large, expensive, new factory or plant, the tax credit 'on this investment could easily outweigh the tax liability for a number of months. The tax credit is as good as cash in the month of purchase. The credit (on investment goods) is available against VAT payable for a period in which the goods were acquired'.[11] The state would be involved in payments, unless it simply allowed the credit to be carried forward. This could be a way to control investment. (See chapter 9.)

This possibility gives rise to a peculiar question about shifting. If a firm's tax credit for capital goods is large enough to annihilate its tax liability for a period or periods, will the firm continue to add the tax content to its price? If we accept that firms pass tax forward fully, then we should argue that when there is no tax liability, prices will be lower than they were when tax was paid.

However, the answer to this probably lies either in the distinction between short run and medium run changes, or in investment policy appraisal. If a firm is already charging prices which include a sales tax, the credit on the purchase of capital goods would only suspend tax liability for a relatively short time. Firms are unwilling to alter price lists in response to every quiver of costs (in a multi-product firm this would involve hundreds of items and very large administrative and printing costs). Therefore, the firm would simply maintain its tax inclusive prices through the period when tax liability was zero.

The alternative is to consider the firm's investment decision. The capital costs will be free of sales tax, but the future earnings will be discounted on the basis of prices which are tax inclusive (if the firm passes sales taxes forward fully). If, in a future period, the prices of goods produced by this capital investment did *not* include the tax passed forward fully because the *total* tax liability of the firm at this future period was outweighed by the capital purchases being made in this period, then the basis on which the *previous* capital investment decision was made would be altered. This is to argue that it is not the current tax credit alone which is relevant for pricing policy, but the previous capital investment decision. In this case, prices would not be altered in the short run in response to the alteration in tax liability occasioned by capital purchase credits.

Where investment goods are used to produce both taxable and non-taxable goods, a simple proportion rule is used and varied according to the ratio of taxed to untaxed turnover averaged over a five-year period.[12]

Changing from purchase tax to the VAT would not have the advantages for investment that Continental countries enjoyed when they switched to the VAT. The cascade tax fell on a wide variety of capital goods and clearly operated against investment. On the other hand, the only capital goods in Britain liable to purchase tax are those bought as inputs by producers of

[11] Organisation for Economic Co-operation and Development, op. cit., p. 190.
[12] Ibid., p. 180–82.

plant and equipment from unregistered businesses. In this way, a tiny amount of double taxation is possible in that purchase tax is paid on the input, and then the capital good produced using that input will have some element of that tax embodied, and when it is used to produce final goods will be liable to purchase tax again.

In both Germany and France, elaborate transitional methods had to be constructed. In Germany, where previously investment goods had been taxed, the state could not afford to relieve such goods of all taxation at once. The credit percentage of 11% VAT was allowed, but an investment tax was then superimposed. Thus in the second half of 1968 a firm might have received 11% credit but paid 8% on an investment good, thereby gaining credit of only 3%. In 1969, the credit remained the same, but the tax was reduced to 7% releasing a net credit of 4%; and so on, until full credit is gained in 1973.

The difficulties in France were not so great as in Germany, as credit had already been given on investment goods. But both goods and persons previously not liable to VAT were now liable. These, combined with the problems of investment goods purchased in previous years, caused quite complicated transitional provisions.

In Britain, transitional problems of this nature would be slight. The loss of revenue from not taxing those investment goods which at present do become liable for purchase tax would be trivial. The advantages to investment would be so slight that no boost to investment could be expected. These changes in the tax liability of capital goods are so minor that transitional provisions for capital goods in Britain would appear unnecessary.

(a) **Both taxes passed forward.** If both taxes are passed forward fully, the tax substitution will not affect investment by a firm (except for the minor items discussed above). Nor would savings be affected except in so far as the tax substitution altered relative prices and hence consumption patterns and, possibly, savings. (See Table 6.3.)

(b) **Both taxes absorbed.** If both taxes are absorbed equally, investment will not be affected. Of course, if a firm decided that the VAT was to be absorbed by wages, whereas the sales tax had been absorbed previously by profits, then there would be an incentive to invest. Equally, the reverse could happen, an investment could be discriminated against. This could differ with each firm. There is no objective criteria which could predetermine the firm's decision in this context.

(c) **VAT passed forward, but other sales taxes absorbed.** But if the VAT which is passed on, replaces other sales taxes which are not, the factors of production are relieved of a tax burden. Once more, the businessman is likely to swing as much as possible of this relief to profits. Investment income will rise and if there were investment opportunities waiting to be undertaken if the rate of return rose, then investment would rise. In macro-economic terms, savings would rise. Of course, all the political and social problems associated with workers real incomes falling and unearned income rising would be repeated here.

(d) VAT absorbed, but other sales taxes passed forward. When the absorbed VAT is substituted for other sales taxes which had been passed on, a tax is imposed on wages and profits. Prices fall, investment returns fall, and it is likely that investment will fall, although it could be argued that there might be a demand for new plant to replace old as inefficient firms attempt to compete. (See the more extended discussion on this point under 'Efficiency' in the next chapter.)

Efficiency

Most of the points raised here are dealt with more satisfactorily in the context of the VAT replacing a profits tax. For the sake of completeness, a brief commentary is included here, but those interested in this problem should read the appropriate section in the next chapter. (See pages 101–103.)

(a) Both taxes passed forward. If the VAT is passed forward fully, it will have no effect on the manner in which firms produce their goods. As the VAT base would be a little wider than that of the present sales taxes, and as it might be less discriminatory (especially if excises were reduced, see chapter 8), consumer preferences will not be as distorted as they are at present. The VAT is more difficult to use as a demand management regulator than the purchase tax. This might reduce the number of times selected industries have to bear sudden tax changes, e.g., car manufacturers. If this created a climate of greater certainty for business decision making, then efficiency might be improved.)

(b) Both taxes absorbed. If the VAT and the conventional sales taxes are absorbed equally, they become taxes on factors. The VAT becomes a tax specifically on profits and wages. Capital goods are exempted, therefore, capital is favoured to wages, and efficiency could be increased. For instance, this could favour the large selfservice shop as compared to a small local retailer. The shop with high capital inputs, low margins, and a smaller ratio of wages to total cost will probably end up with a lower tax liability per item sold than the wide margin, large wage bill, local store. The introduction of the VAT could, therefore, encourage efficiency in retailing, but at the expense of a traditional way of selling goods through small local outlets. In this case, the VAT is actually speeding up a process which is already operating. Indeed, many of the larger retailers in France, e.g., Monoprix and Prisunic, favoured the introduction of the VAT.

Basically, if the VAT and the sales taxes it replaces are both passed forward, there is no gain in efficiency through the change. If both are equally absorbed, there are possible efficiency gains. There is no loss in the one case and a possible gain in the other. Nothing to lose and something to gain: it is the basis for a good bet.

The crucial point is whether the tax is passed forward. As both are truly general, it seems likely in the light of the previous discussion that they will be passed forward. But as competition under the EEC increases, the more efficient firms (capital intensive, using new machinery, etc.—see below) might prefer to absorb the taxes to gain competitive advantage. Efficiency gained from the tax substitution would then be reaped. This argument is extended, with all the *caveats* and possibilities explored, in the next chapter.

(c) VAT passed forward, but other sales taxes absorbed. If the VAT is passed forward and other sales taxes are absorbed, a tax on all factors is removed and one on consumption imposed. There is no spur to efficiency. In fact, as profits will be easier to achieve, there may be a diminution of efficiency.

(d) VAT absorbed, but other sales taxes passed forward. With the reverse, a tax on consumption is removed and a tax on wages (and profits) is imposed: this will be likely to increase efficiency. (See Table 6.2.)

Balance of payments

Wholesale and retail sales taxes are not paid on exports. Under the VAT, the tax content of an export is fully rebated. In both cases, the good is exported free of tax.

(a) Both taxes passed forward. If the wholesale and retail taxes are passed forward fully, there is no difference between the two taxes and their effect on exports. The same is true of imports. Both taxes will tax imports at the full rate commensurate with similar domestically produced goods. In this way, substituting one tax for another should have no effect on the balance of payments.

(b) Both taxes absorbed. If the taxes are not passed forward fully, substituting a tax which could be rebated for one which cannot, might help exports. But this is subject to six restrictive assumptions discussed in detail in the next chapter. It is most important that these conditions should be fully appreciated before any effect on the balance of payments can be identified (pages 103–108).

(c) VAT passed forward, but other sales taxes absorbed. If the VAT is passed on and other sales taxes absorbed, the substitution will increase domestic prices and reduce the competitive advantage of domestic exports. Imports would be at a relative advantage compared with the position before the tax substitution.

(d) VAT absorbed, but other sales taxes passed forward. In the opposite case, prices fall and the country's international competitive position is improved. (See Table 6.3.)

There are two further points to be mentioned about exports, imports, and businesses. First, there might be a slight psychological difference between the two taxes. Value added tax is actually a claim when the good is exported. The money in the exporter's hand may give him a mental boost on an export order. It is true that the exporter under the retail and wholesale sales taxes gets no such rebate. On the other hand, he works with tax free materials and is not obliged to make a month long interest free loan to the government. If he passes the tax forward fully, then of course, there is no burden of tax upon him, and no loan to the government. In this case, if the loan is made by anyone, it is by the public who buy the goods. Under the VAT, it is possible to avoid the interest free loan to the government if the exporter obtains his materials tax free for the goods he intends to export. This is done in France (known as the *regime suspensif*), where tax free material for exports can be obtained up to the value of the previous year's exports by the firm. In Britain, the manufacturer who exports all his products at the moment obviously pays no purchase tax, but under the VAT he would be liable for tax on inputs and not be able to claim credit for tax on materials used until he exported. This lag would probably force him to expand his working capital. It might be worth considering some adaptation of the French *regime suspensif* in Britain to meet this specific problem. But if the VAT is, in any part, absorbed, there is a psychological boost. There is also a very real money cost in the enforced loan to the government. On balance, the VAT comes off worse.

A second point is that the VAT could discourage imports if importers had to pay the tax at the moment the goods were imported, while a purchase from a domestic producer created a tax liability which had to be settled, say, a month later. As an indication of the scale of this problem, Denmark 'attempted to favour neither imported nor domestic products by charging the former at a lower rate (7% instead of 10%) at the importation stage'.[13] Presumably, this lower rate at importation did not mean a final lower tax liability for the class of goods, but simply that 'catching up' took place at the stage after importation. All other countries require the tax to be paid at the time of importation and it would seem sensible for other countries introducing the VAT to do the same. Any discrimination against the importer, favouring the domestic producer, would tend to help the balance of payments.

[13] Organisation for Economic Co-operation and Development, op. cit., p. 30.

Summary

(a) A survey of theory and empirical evidence indicates that sales taxes are largely, but not always entirely, shifted forwards.

(b) If both taxes are passed forward there is no advantage (Table 6.3, column 1).

(c) If the taxes are equally absorbed (Table 6.3, column 2), the current balance of payments could improve, investment might increase, and prices would not rise.

(d) One of these options offers a no change position and the other a possible gain. In column 1, nothing is lost and, if things turn out as in column 2, something might be won and little stands to be lost (a possible slight fall in real wages and profits).

Table 6.3

Summary of the effects of VAT replacing sales taxes

Real changes in	All taxes passed forward	All taxes equally absorbed	VAT passed forward sales tax absorbed	VAT absorbed sales tax passed forward
Prices	O/+	O	+	−
Profits	O	O/−	+	−
Wages	O	O/−	O	+
Investment	O	O/+	+	−
Efficiency	O	+	O/−	+
Output	O	+	O	+
Balance of payments				
Exports	O	O/+	−	+
Imports	O	O	+	−
X–M	O	O/+	−	+

(e) The options shown in columns 3 and 4 are unlikely combinations. The current wholesale and retail sales taxes are not absorbed, therefore, column 3 in unlikely to be a possible position for Britain.

(f) When the turnover and wholesale taxes are passed forward (column 4) the substitution of VAT is much more likely to result in the effects in column 1 than those in column 4. However, if at least part of the VAT were substituted for the tax on *profits*, as well as the turnover and wholesale taxes, then some of the effects of column 4 might occur. This is discussed in the next chapter.

(g) A VAT fully payable immediately on goods imported could discriminate against imports.

Recommendation for countries considering adopting the VAT

It is likely that conventional sales taxes are substantially shifted forwards; substituting the VAT for these taxes would probably encourage forward shifting. The most likely assumptions to be realized in practice are those in Table 6.3, column 1. This would mean no significant change in prices, profits, wages, investment, efficiency, output, or in the balance of payments. If, however, the VAT were absorbed, even partially, then prices might fall, the balance of payments could improve, but profits and investment might fall. Therefore, the case for adopting the VAT must lie outside the effects of this differential incidence.

7. The value added tax replacing profits tax: effects on prices, investment, efficiency, and the balance of payments

General discussion

Let us assume that the VAT is substituted for a tax on profits; or alternatively, that the VAT replaces other sales taxes but at a rate sufficiently high to yield an excess revenue which is used to reduce profits taxation. In either case, direct profits tax liability is reduced.

As in the previous chapter, most of the argument turns on whether the VAT and the profits tax are passed forward or not. At this point, economic theory and some empirical evidence contradict one another. This is not unusual, but demands some discussion and, if possible, explanation.

Theory has always held that firms seek to maximize profits. Whether the government takes a larger or smaller portion of the profits will not alter the firm's profit maximization and, therefore, cannot alter prices. A gloss has been added to this simple presentation by arguing that firms earn widely different amounts of profits depending on their efficiency, information, etc. But the 'marginal' firm (or the 'marginal unit of production' of other firms) earns no profit and, therefore, profits will not be affected by a profits tax, i.e., a profits tax on zero profits cannot affect prices.

Some empirical studies show this to be untrue in practice. In the US Musgrave and Krzyaniak[1] found forward shifting of over 100% of profits taxes. The kernel of the Royal Commission's rejection of the VAT was that the substitution of a tax which would be passed forward[2] for one which was not (the Corporation Tax), must increase prices. The increased prices would decrease the competitive position of exports and the balance of payments

[1] Musgrave R. A. and Krzyaniak M: *The Shifting of the Corporation Tax*, Johns Hopkins Press, Baltimore, 1962.
[2] The Richardson Committee, op. cit., Chaps. 8 and 9.

on current account would deteriorate. Increased wage demands to maintain real wages would increase costs and this would further decrease the international competitive position of exports. Of course, implicit in this statement is the suggestion that British firms do not take profits taxes into account at all when fixing prices and therefore, do not pass forward profits tax changes in prices. On the other hand, another British survey indicated at least partial forward shifting of profits taxes.[3]

The reasons for these contradictory results and the conflict with traditional theory can be presented in seven arguments.

(a) **Business pricing methods.** Businessmen may not maximize profits. They may prefer a quiet life with adequate profit, they may seek to maximize turnover, or a long run rate of return; they may prefer to be the market leader in terms of size. In such cases, with profits below an optimum, space is left for discretionary price changes consequent on tax changes. In Britain, businessmen may often prefer to have a guaranteed quiet existence compared to maximum profit. I have already commented (chapter 6) that in a highly protected market profits may not be maximized to avoid antagonizing the government, attracting undue attention to tariff protection, etc.

(b) **General state of the economy.** If trading conditions are buoyant and markets are expanding, then profits tax increases are more likely to be passed on while decreases are less likely to be passed on. In an inflationary environment, all firms find it possible to pass forward taxes in the long run. Simply, as all prices are changing, price comparisons become difficult, people come to expect price increases and regard them as normal, and traders seek to recoup taxes when they change their prices.

(c) **Investment decision making.** If firms actually make investment decisions without taking account of taxation then, of course, all government designs to induce business investment by tax concessions are pointless. Yet businessmen maintain that such investment incentives are not without effect. This smacks of having your cake and eating it. If businessmen actually take their investment decisions without assessing taxation or grants then all the sophisticated methods of discounted-cash-flow look irrelevant. In fact businesses probably do take account of taxes and grants, but only sporadically and in a crude manner. Thus a specific tax change might not immediately be reflected in a price change, but might influence future pricing and investment policy. Moreover, the NEDO report[4] claimed: 'The growing sophistication of business accounting procedures is resulting in closer attention being paid to post-tax profitability.' So that eventually tax changes might affect pricing policy.

[3] Mackintosh, A. S: *The Development of Firms*, Cambridge University Press, 1963.
[4] NEDO: *Value Added Tax*, op. cit., para. 5.41 and p. 90, A44.

(d) Elasticity of demand and supply. As in chapter 6, a producer faced by an elastic demand curve may be reluctant to raise prices, and particularly so if his own costs are decreasing with increased output. The increase in price would reduce demand and hence raise his costs.

(e) Size of profits. If profits are a very small percentage of total turnover, then the burden of the tax will be small in relation to the prices of individual commodities. Indeed this is true of all changes in profits taxation. To recoup the increased tax from increased commodity prices often involves a very small change in final prices, for example, if a firm's profits were 20% of a turnover of £100 000 and each unit sold for 50p, a tax of 10% on profits would require an increase in selling price of about 1p, i.e., 2%. As most company tax changes are of smaller magnitude then 10% and often the unit price is less than 50p, the change in unit price needed to recoup the tax is often negligible. Businesses may delay changing prices until a combination of cost increases forces their hand. A rise in raw material costs, and then a wage increase might not cause a company to change prices in the short run; but a tax increase on top of these might oblige the company to recoup the entire combination of costs through increased selling prices. Thus the tax increase may get the blame for the price increase, which is in fact covering a backlog of cost increases. Alternatively, a tax change may be absorbed for a time until some other cost increase obliges the firm to revise its price list.

(f) Size of the tax change. The survey conducted by the NEDO committee[5] indicated that a *substantial* cut in corporation tax might allow an equal yield in VAT to be substituted without a rise in prices. In practice, the possibility of a large cut in corporation profits tax looks remote.[6] Three reasons are given for not making a large switch from corporation profits tax to VAT. None of the reasons seems particularly valid.

First, the corporation profits tax has only recently been introduced and it is held that it should not be altered. This is a weak reason for not changing it. Many economists have doubts about the theoretical validity of the reasoning behind the introduction of the corporation profits tax. To argue that a tax should not be changed because it is new sounds like an easy way out.

Second, to argue that the substitution would be a switch from direct to indirect taxation and, therefore, socially undesirable appears to miss the whole point of the discussion of shifting. If the VAT is in fact not shifted forward in higher prices, then it becomes a tax on factors, i.e., a direct tax. If the substantial cut in corporation profits tax and substitution of an equal yield VAT resulted in a straightforward tax replacement with no change in prices then, in effect, a direct tax has been substituted for a direct tax. To argue that a substantial reduction would involve a greater switch from the

[5] NEDO: *Value Added Tax*, op. cit., para. 5.41.
[6] Ibid., para. 5.43.

direct taxation of corporate profits to the indirect taxation of goods and services[7] is a confusion of terms and effects.

Third, to argue that corporate taxes are not high in Britain by international standards and that the substitution would make them even lower, is open to the same criticism as above (that the VAT *could* fall on profits). A further criticism is that if the change is desirable on *economic* grounds should it be shelved because it puts Britain out-of-line with others? The point remains that a substantial cut in the corporation profits tax might allow an equal yield VAT to be absorbed, a small cut would probably encourage the forward shifting of the VAT.

(g) **Form of the tax and government attitude.** There seems little doubt that the French form of VAT is designed to encourage forward shifting. Indeed, the Commission repeatedly refers to the VAT as a sales tax and assumes it to be passed forward. In these circumstances, it is hardly surprising that firms pass the VAT on in their prices.

It is clear no definite statement can be made on this issue of the shifting of corporate taxes. But the discussion does indicate that it would be most reasonable to assume that profits tax changes are passed forward—though not necessarily at once. It should be mentioned that unincorporated businesses would not benefit from a cut in profits taxes. Unless it was deliberate policy to discriminate against such firms, the logical corollary to a reduction in profits taxation would be a cut in personal income tax.

To cover all possible combinations, when considering an equal yield VAT replacing company profits tax, the discussion will again consider the alternative assumptions:

(a) That both the VAT and the profits tax are passed forward fully.
(b) That both the VAT and the profits tax are fully absorbed.
(c) That the VAT is passed forward, but the profits tax is absorbed.
(d) That the VAT is absorbed, but the profits tax is passed forward.

A summary, in tabular form, is presented at the end of the chapter. (See Table 7.1.)

Prices

(a) **Both taxes passed forward.** If both the VAT and the profits tax are passed forward, the effect on prices will be negligible. Presumably there will be changes in relative prices as firms which have high profits and low turnovers tend to lower prices. The high profits would have attracted a high profits tax, this is removed and replaced by a tax on the small turnover and the tax liability is reduced; therefore, if the tax liability is passed on in each case in price changes, the substitution will cause prices to fall. While those with low profits and high turnovers will increase prices. The final result on the cost of living will depend on the various household consumption patterns for

[7] Ibid., para. 5.42.

goods and services whose relative prices have changed. But in any case, although prices might remain the same, rise, or fall, the total movement is unlikely to be large.

(b) **Both taxes absorbed.** If the VAT is absorbed then it becomes a tax on wages and profits. This is contrasted to a tax on profits alone which it is replacing. Naturally prices will be unchanged. The tax will now fall on two factors of production—labour and capital, whereas the profits tax had only fallen on capital. If prices do not change, then the real rewards to both factors are reduced. Relative to the previous position, however, the burden is spread over two factors rather than one and, therefore, profits will be better off and wages worse. This tax change assumption, therefore, is likely to have a regressive effect.

(c) **VAT passed forward, but profits tax absorbed.** If the VAT is passed on and the profits tax it replaces has been absorbed, then a tax on factors is replaced by a tax on consumption. This is the Richardson Commission's argument. Prices would be increased and the reward to capital owners would rise. This combination would be likely to trigger a series of wage demands as workers fought to maintain their real wages. These cost increases would lead to another round of price increases affecting the international competitive position of exports.

(d) **VAT absorbed, but profits tax passed forward.** When the VAT is absorbed it becomes a tax on wages, salaries, and profits, but replaces a profits tax which was passed on, therefore prices fall. However, the VAT on wages and profits would reduce money incomes and the real gain would depend on the household mix of incomes from wages and dividends, and the consumption pattern of goods at the reduced prices.

On this question of prices, it is worth mentioning that Kaldor reckoned that a VAT of 10% replacing the British profits tax (as it then was), the income tax on undistributed profits, *and* the purchase tax, might only raise final prices by some 1% to 2%. Nevertheless, this small price increase would be accompanied by:

> a considerable shift in the burden of taxation from the owners of enterprise, to wage and salary earners; a shift that would manifest itself, not so much in a reduction in real wages and salaries, but in the failure of real wages to rise with the consequential rise in average productivity and in the rise in the share of profits. It would thus increase the inequality in the distribution of income, which would become further enhanced with the passage of time. For it would greatly speed up the accumulation of personal for tunes by men who are successful in business and thereby promote an even greater concentration in the ownership of wealth. It would also augment the share of national resources devoted to luxury consumption. From an equity point of view or a socio-political point of view, such a

change could therefore only be contemplated if it were coupled with a considerable increase in the range and effectiveness of the taxation of personal wealth, e.g., by the introduction of a progressive wealth tax, an effective tax on capital gains and a gift tax—and possibly by some restraint (by means of a special tax or other means) on increases in dividend payments.[8]

From another point of view, the vintage argument claims that profits taxation does affect prices (contrasted to the traditional theoretical view that it does not). A reduction of profits tax (substituting the VAT) could enable those firms which are price leaders and which tend to have the most modern equipment, to accept a lower gross return on capital presently employed, prices could be reduced, and firms with the oldest (least efficient) machinery would have to re-equip to obtain comparable profits. Investment projects which up till the profits tax reduction had not been attractive enough to undertake would now become attractive, and new (more modern) investment would occur. After all, this is one of the justifications for the downward sloping, rightward, investment schedule.

This would occur (if prices work this way) if the profits tax were reduced independently of the VAT being absorbed or passed on (cases (a) to (d)). The maximum effect would be if the VAT were fully passed on and profits tax were wholly reflected in price changes (column 1, Table 7.2.) On the other hand, even if the VAT were absorbed, as the yield would be spread over both profits and wages, the rate on profits would be likely to be lower than that now on profits. Once again, profits taxes would be reduced.

Investment

As far as the tax free treatment of investment goods is concerned, company profits tax and the VAT are dissimilar. Depreciation under profits taxation on a historical basis (and FIFO for stocks) penalizes re-equipment during an inflation. Full immediate credit against VAT tax liability on investment goods would penalize the company only in so far as it makes interest free loans to the government for a time, but abolition of profits tax will remove historical allowances for capital depreciation. The net effect of this change would be a substantial once and for all boost to new investment. Although when using the plant, the depreciation and interest create taxable value added, and there is a postponement of tax liability.

Any decision similar to the French 'buffer rule' which does not allow net tax credits to be refunded by the state, and obliges firms to continue to carry net tax credits forward until exhausted, can penalize investment. A new firm, or a firm investing in a lot of capital equipment, is obliged to make an interest free loan to the government. Clearly, if one of the advantages of the VAT is to encourage investment, this 'buffer rule' which operates against the new and fast expanding firm, reduces the attractiveness of the tax.

[8] Kaldor, N: *Essays on Economic Policy*, Volume 1, Duckworth, 1964, p. 288.

(a) **Both taxes passed forward.** If the VAT replaces a profits tax and both are passed forward there is no effect on investment policies.

(b) **Both taxes absorbed.** The tax on profits is replaced by a tax on wages and profits. Prices are unchanged but the real returns to capital rise and those to labour fall. If unions are successful in restoring the real wages of their members, yet firms do not (or cannot) raise prices, then firms with a higher ratio of labour to output will be penalized compared to more capital intensive firms. This could be an incentive to investment.

(c) **VAT passed forward, but profits tax absorbed.** Profits of companies increase by the full amount of the tax relief, while prices rise by the full amount of the new tax. Although the prices of capital goods rise as well as other prices, businesses can offset the tax embodied in capital goods against their own VAT liability. They are thereby fully compensated for the price change in capital inputs. But if the general rise in prices for other goods results in demands for increased wages which are met, then the cost of wages as an input rises relative to capital. Once more this is an incentive to investment. This is the case made by the NEDO report.[9] It is worth pointing out a further twist to this argument. If wages rise this will include a cost increase in the capital goods industries which they will try to recoup through higher prices. The extent that the prices of capital goods rise due to the secondary increase in wages will offset the net advantage of capital to labour and reduce the incentive to invest to all industry.

(d) **VAT absorbed, but profits tax passed forward.** Prices should fall, but the rewards to factors will be reduced. Profits will bear tax whereas previously they did not. Real wages should rise (prices should fall by more than the reduction in wages). The reduced reward to capital would discourage investment.

It should be pointed out that, as argued at the end of the chapter in Table 7.2, the possibilities (b) to (d) above which affect investment are all less likely to occur in practice than assumption (a) which would have no effect on investment.

Even under assumptions (b) and (c) there is a particular case, which is widespread, which might affect investment adversely. Where companies earn smaller or zero profits, the profits tax has no effect on them, but the imposition of the VAT extends their potential tax base to include wages. Where the VAT is passed on there is no change in the analysis ((a) and (c) above). But when the VAT is absorbed wages are taxed where previously they were not. This could discriminate against labour and in favour of capital, for example, in most nationalized industries. Of course, if profits were earned, they would become liable to tax as well, but the change is between a position where no tax liability is incurred to one where it is created. Capital goods

[9] NEDO: *Value Added Tax*, op. cit., para. 5.32.

inputs could be purchased tax free (because of the credit offset) but labour would be relatively more expensive than capital.

On the macro-economic side of investment and savings, with taxes on profits reduced or abolished, even if the volume of dividend distribution does not change, there would be an increase in the amount of dividends net of tax. This in itself could raise investment, as the flow of funds available for investment would be increased. If dividends were distributed, they accrue to high income households with low marginal propensities to consume and the demand for goods would not increase substantially. If, at the same time, the VAT was passed on in higher prices (Table 7.2, column 3) the lower income households would find their real incomes falling. The social and political consequences of such a combination would be awkward.

Total savings would probably increase, but at the same time the total domestic market might have shrunk due to falling real incomes of high marginal propensity to consume households. The smaller market might not offer investment opportunities sufficient to absorb the increased flow of funds.

The overall effect of a VAT fully passed on substituted for a profits tax might be an economy with higher prices and manufacturers looking for profitable investments to take advantage of the lower profits taxes. As the domestic market would have contracted due to the higher prices, the more profitable investment might have to be found overseas and this could be a help to exports (see below). Of course, as capital is internationally a most mobile factor, this combination could simply push capital overseas instead of increasing investment in exporting industries especially with the free capital movement within the EEC.

Efficiency

As mentioned above, if the VAT which replaces the profits tax is absorbed, (cases (b) and (d)), then it becomes a tax on *wages* and profits. This factor tax may then encourage the 'best' use of labour.

If a company makes no profits it pays no tax; yet it may be continuing to operate on a large scale, employing many persons. In a capitalist economy, profits can be the yardstick of efficiency, and it could be held that a company employing many people, using large amounts of raw materials, yet making no profits, is behaving inefficiently. The resources of raw materials and man-power it is using could be put to better use in companies which make a profit. Thus a VAT which creates a tax liability even if no profits are made, i.e., it becomes a payroll tax, forces the company to economize on labour and to make profits from which it can meet its tax liability.

This could have momentous effects on industry. Some nationalized industries make little profits yet have large wage bills, e.g., British Railways. These bodies would be liable for a substantial payroll tax substituted for their negligible liability to profits taxation. This might be no bad thing.

However, it should be clearly recognized that such a move could have far reaching effects on labour employment. Firms not so dramatically placed as those mentioned above might find a considerable incentive to economize on labour and this is probably desirable in terms of efficiency and labour productivity.

This labour substitution effect would be reinforced as the VAT element in the price of capital goods would be fully credited against VAT liability, thus capital goods relative to labour would be in a favourable position. But since capital goods are produced by labour, and labour cannot be produced by capital, the costs of production by capital intensive methods would be likely to rise by the same percentage as the cost of producing by labour intensive methods.

If the VAT were not absorbed (cases (a) and (c)), then the case where the profits tax was also passed forward would produce changes in relative prices. But as there is no obvious correlation between the size of profit relative to turnover and the wage bill, it is impossible to say whether there would be a bias towards 'efficiency'. Where there were obvious companies with large turnovers and no profit (again British Railways), clearly prices would rise relative to other companies. This could reduce demand for the product and either force 'efficiency' in that firm, or direct the resources to firms that could use them more efficiently.

If the VAT was passed on and the profits tax absorbed, then the firms making the biggest profits would suffer the largest price increases. There would be no incentive to 'efficiency' in this case.

Of course, profits in themselves need not be the measurement of efficiency. Low profits instead of reflecting inefficiency might simply be the result of cyclical influences, or they may be temporary due to starting new plant, or even arise because the firm is new and has not yet earned substantial profits. Large profits, on the other hand, could be the result of protected monopolies producing inefficiently. Moreover, lower taxation of profits and an increased flow of cash do not necessarily result in increased sensible investment. Retained profits could be misused in nationally valueless ventures. However, given capitalist orientated European economies (omitting the nationalized industries), it is probably reasonable to use profits as a yardstick of efficiency.

Of course, all this discussion would be of less importance if businessmen made their investment decisions ignoring taxes and subsidies. This was the tenor of the replies by businessmen to the Richardson Committee. Influences other than taxation (improvement in product quality, cost reduction, marketing), bulked much larger in investment decisions than taxation. Also, numerous alterations in government rulings on taxes and investment have made business wary of taking long run decisions on the basis of such variable conditions. Nevertheless, a fundamental change in government tax policy involving the abolition or reduction of a familiar tax, and the introduction of an entirely new one, would almost certainly cause a re-appraisal by many businesses of their labour/capital ratios.

A secondary, more roundabout encouragement to efficiency comes from modern plants having a higher profit margin, relative to sales than old plants. The reduction or abolition of profits tax should mean a larger gain to the modern plant while both the old and modern plants are liable for the same VAT. As older plants tend to employ more labour, i.e., are less efficient, this taxation switch would encourage the transfer of labour from the less profitable old plant to the new. This improves efficiency and productivity.

In so far as more efficient management can be identified with modern labour saving methods of production, the changeover would tend to concentrate resources in the hands of the more efficient.

These arguments depend on the assumption that those firms using modern methods increase their prices relative to wages by less than the full amount of the VAT (cases (b) and (d)). This puts the pressure on the older, labour intensive plants. If the VAT is passed on fully, the relative positions of the two plants are unchanged.

The tradition of protected domestic markets, often dominated by a few family businesses, has sometimes in small countries bred a cosy attitude towards business taxation. Any tax on companies in these circumstances might be passed on. This will reduce the impact of the VAT on efficiency. On the other hand, the reduction of tariffs, the fight for export markets, the decline of the family firm, and the opening up of the domestic market, could well oblige firms to be less cavalier in their treatment of company taxation. These influences might encourage, at least partial, absorption of the VAT with consequent effects on efficiency.

Balance of payments

This is a complicated and delicate area. Some simple accounts of the VAT indicate that there are advantages for exporters in this tax. This simple statement is unlikely to be true. First, let us look at the straightforward attitude, and then discuss the necessary qualifications.

The OECD, GATT, and the Treaty of Rome all forbid subsidies to exporters. Therefore, no corporate tax remission, as presently given in, for example, Northern Ireland, could be granted to exporters.

Sales taxes can be remitted. Retail sales taxes are obviously not payable on exports; nor is the purchase tax. Even if sales taxes were levied at stages of production before the wholesale tax, they could be remitted if they could be accurately calculated. Of course, the calculation of the tax content of any price becomes more difficult as the taxation of successive stages mounts. The tax content of a good taxed under a cascade tax cannot be known accurately, thus the remissions of this tax usually involve either a hidden subsidy or penalty. This was a problem Germany faced. It is the peculiar, and principal, virtue of the Continental VAT that the sales tax content of a price is always easily known. So the VAT is always fully rebatable upon exports. The simple statement becomes, therefore, as the VAT is rebatable on exports, and corporate income taxes are not, the replacement of company income taxes by VAT must help exporters.

Such optimism is most misleading. It depends on at least six assumptions:

(a) The first assumption is that corporate income taxes are reflected in higher export prices which would be reduced if the tax were removed. If corporate income taxes are not reflected in higher export prices, then British companies are at no disadvantage compared to countries using the VAT. Of course, if there is considerable profits tax remission on exports already, as in many small countries, profits taxes are clearly not reflected in export prices, therefore, the abolition of profits taxes would have no effect. But even looking ahead, or at those exports where remission is not earned, the extent to which corporate taxes are shifted is most controversial. Recent research, as mentioned earlier, suggests a substantial amount of shifting. Equally, the evidence suggests a selfish, myopic approach to taxes by businesses; when taxes rise they pass them on, when they fall they do not.

(b) Even if we accept that corporate income taxes are passed on, they may not be passed on to export prices. Where export markets are difficult, cross subsidization of exports by domestic sales (dumping) may occur. In this way, a firm may make a loss on export sales even though covering marginal cost. Under a profits tax, this loss can be offset against the profits tax liability incurred on domestic sales. With the VAT as a sales tax there cannot be an offset against domestic tax liability for losses made on sales abroad. Thus to raise the equivalent tax revenue from the VAT, the tax rate on domestic sales would have to be higher.[10] The position might be summed up by saying that under the profits tax you can have a negative tax liability (losses); under a sales tax you cannot have negative sales. With the VAT, the tax liability on exports is zero, but that is still not as good as a negative tax liability to offset against domestic tax liabilities. In this way, exports might be reduced.

(c) Even when corporate income taxes are passed forward, if other countries with corporate income taxes (and *all* of the EEC countries have such taxes, 15% in Italy, Germany 51%, upon undistributed and 23·5% upon distributed profits, France 50%, the Netherlands 43% to 58%) pass these forward, then there is no net difference between Britain and the other countries. The only question would be whether the British sales taxes were fully remitted on exports com-

[10] Rybczynski, T. M., Ed: *The Value Added Tax: the U.K. Position and the European Experience*, Basil Blackwell, Oxford, 1969, p. 58.

pared to countries which fully remitted the VAT. The answer is that a very small part of the purchase tax spills over and is included in export sales (perhaps $2\frac{1}{2}\%$ of purchase tax revenue), and this will, in a miniscule way, increase export prices, and is not rebatable. But such a difference is slight.

(d) To gain an advantage, the demand for exports should be relatively elastic. If the demand is inelastic, the fall in price will only produce lower money values for the same volume of goods exported before the change. The advantages gained from devaluation indicate that Britain does enjoy an elastic demand for exports. But with a smaller, more agricultural country, like Ireland or Denmark, agricultural exports are not necessarily a function of price, but of subsidies both foreign and domestic, and it is difficult to see much advantage for these. In evidence to the NEDO, many firms stressed that small price reductions were of limited significance in capturing export markets. More important were prompt delivery, quality, variety, design, etc.

(e) Exports sales would gain a maximum increase if prices fell relative to the countries who compete with British goods in British export markets. If other countries reduce their prices in answer to the British price reduction, Britain would be no better off.

(f) Finally, if the corporate income tax is absorbed and the VAT is passed on (Table 7.2, column 3, which is what the Richardson Committee thought would happen), the rise in domestic prices could trigger off wage demands and the ensuing inflation would annihilate any competitive advantage of British exports. Indeed, the Richardson Committee thought this was so likely that it would leave British exports in a worse position than previously. The ability of companies to pass on the VAT would be limited by competition. With the advent of the EEC, competition might force businesses to absorb the VAT thus limiting the price rise, and at the same time, producing those cost efficiency results discussed above.

When we take account of all these special considerations, the original shine of the simple statement becomes rather tarnished. It now reads that since the VAT is rebatable on exports and corporate income taxation is not, the replacement of the corporate tax by a VAT will help exports if corporate income tax, which is not at present rebated is reflected in higher prices for exports which are reduced when the corporate income tax is reduced. Other countries with corporate income taxes should have their tax passed forward at a higher level than the same tax in Britain. The demand for exports should be elastic, and other countries should not retaliate against the British price reduction. Most important of all, the imposition of the VAT must not spark off a domestic wage/price spiral to erode the competitive price of exports.

The statement on the expected improvement in exports is not particularly exciting or convincing. Kaldor calculated that if a VAT replaced the profits tax, it would bring about an advantage equal to a general reduction in wages of $2\frac{1}{2}\%$ to $3\frac{1}{2}\%$.[11] Whereas, Stout reckoned that inflation would result if a company tax of 50% were removed and a VAT of 10% substituted for profits and purchase taxes since prices in Britain would increase by 3% to 4%, thus wiping out the potential gain. 'If price-setters ignore profits tax relief and all shift the tax fully by raising prices all along the line . . . and if at the same time wages did not change, then the benefit to exports would disappear, except in the sense that relief from purchase tax benefits exports'.[12] If wages did rise in step with the rise in prices attributable to the VAT, then theoretically, this should be a once and for all increase in prices and wages and could leave 'discrimination in favour of mechanization, buying-in (specialist suppliers), rapid investment growth, and profitability'.[13] Unfortunately, doubt persists whether the price/wage change could be contained to a neat once and for all increase. It could well trigger off the familiar cumulative wage reaction based on leapfrogging comparative claims.

There is an extension to this argument. It can be argued that the more direct corporate taxes you replace by the VAT, the more you relieve exports of taxation. For example, if all employers' social security payments in Britain were abolished and met from VAT receipts, companies that export would no longer have to include social security payments in their export prices. The VAT to cover these charges would be completely rebated on the exports.

But this concentration on the micro-economic effects ignores important macro-economic elements and is thereby misleading. The points for and against are similar to those argued above. If companies pass forward the social security contributions and reflect their abolition in a price reduction, the VAT would replace this and would have to be at a rate higher than the reduction of social security contributions, because it would not be obtained from all sales, only from domestic sales. Therefore, domestic prices would rise (the VAT would increase prices more than the abolition of social security contributions would reduce them). Once more, the price rise could trigger off wage demands and reduce the internationally competitive position of exports. Again, the eventual success of any export price reduction depends on the elasticity of demand for exports and on the policy of other countries.

The discussion is the same for other taxes which might be replaced by the VAT. Throughout Europe there is the problem of *taxe occulte* especially in relation to the tax on hydrocarbon oil. The *taxe occulte* is simply the tax content in goods or services used as inputs for further production which cannot be reclaimed under the VAT. Obviously, in Britain the excise on hydrocarbon oils is paid by companies for the transport of their goods and

[11] Kaldor, N: op. cit., p. 291.
[12] Stout, D. K. and Turvey, R: 'Value Added Taxation, Exporting and Growth', *British Tax Review*, September/October 1962, p. 329.
[13] Ibid., p. 330.

thereby enters into the cost of production and hence increases export prices. If this excise were removed and the lost revenue replaced by a VAT, then producers could recoup the tax content on their inputs of hydrocarbon oils, and the tax would be recouped entirely on exports equivalent to approximately 2 % of turnover.[14]

From Table 7.1, it will be seen that hydrocarbon oils represent about £700 million in terms of intermediate expenditure. Rates are even larger at £758 million. Motor vehicle licences and the SET also bulk large. Now it would be perfectly possible to abolish all these taxes and recoup the revenue by using the VAT. However, attractive as that seems at the micro-economic level, and attractive as it seems to the businessman, it is doubtful whether the case is any different to those argued above.

Table 7.1

Taxe opaque **in Britain 1969**

Type of tax	Total revenue £ million	*Taxe opaque* £ million	*Taxe opaque* as a % of total revenue
Hydrocarbon oils	1267	696	55
Purchase tax	1108	88	8
Motor vehicle licences	428	190	44
SET	808	182	23
Stamp duties	123	50	41
Rates	1674	758	45
All expenditure taxes	7868	2131	27
Total	13276	4095	31

Source: Adapted from Economic Trends, Nov. 1970. p. xxvii/viii.

If the government wishes to maintain its revenue, then the VAT on the more limited tax base (excluding exports) will have to be at a higher rate than the excise it replaces. The discussion then proceeds as previously: the higher domestic prices will spark off wage increases and the international competitive advantage will be eroded.

Overall, it could be argued that if a dramatic tax change were made, substituting VAT for corporate income taxation, this could encourage businesses to reduce their prices for exports. In our main markets for exports, companies may also pass forward a substantial part of their tax liabilities. The demand for our exports may be price elastic. All these points favour a beneficial effect on exports of the tax substitution.

But we are not sure how far manufactuers pass taxes forward, nor do we know with certainty the price elasticities of our exports. However, we do

[14] NEDO, *Value Added Tax*, op. cit., para. 5.71.

know that the trade unions in Britain are well organized and would certainly attempt to maintain the real wages of their members, and this could well erode any small advantage achieved for the balance of payments by the substitution of VAT.

On the import side, the VAT would be imposed at a rate comparable to the VAT content of domestically produced goods at the same stage of production. In so far as domestically produced goods rose in price because of a higher VAT content, so imports would be charged with higher taxes. Their relative position should remain unchanged.

Summary

Table 7.2

Summary of the effects of VAT replacing profits tax

Real changes in	All taxes passed forward	All taxes equally absorbed	VAT passed on, profits tax absorbed	VAT absorbed, profits tax passed on
Prices	−/O/+	O/−	+	−
Profits	+	+	+	−
Wages	O	−	−	+
Investment	+	+	+	−
Efficiency	O/+	O/+	O/+	+
Output	O	+	O	+/−
Balance of payments				
Exports	O/+	O/+	−	+
Imports	O	O	O	O
X–M	O/+	O/+	−	+

(a) A review of the theoretical position indicated that it was reasonable to assume that profits tax changes (especially upwards) are passed forward, though not necessarily at once.
(b) A VAT replacing a tax on profits could reduce prices and increase investment by encouraging the replacement of old plant.
(c) Dividends might be increased and total savings could rise, but this might pose awkward problems for trade unions and incomes policies.
(d) If absorbed, the VAT would be a tax on wages and this would have profound effects on some firms, particularly those with low profits and high wage bills, e.g., nationalized industries.
(f) Capital intensive plant investment might be encouraged.
(g) The effects on the balance of payments of the VAT replacing a tax on company profits are complicated and uncertain. In British circumstances the substitution might be favourable, but could be vitiated by domestic inflation from a price/wage spiral.

(h) The least likely assumptions are those in column 4 of Table 7.2. The other columns indicate that most of the effects of a VAT replacing the profits tax would be either neutral or favourable, except that real wages might be reduced and this, in turn, produces problems of wage demands which negate any or all of the other advantages.

Relevance to Britain

The most likely assumptions to apply to Britain are those in column 1 in Table 7.2. In this case, there *could* be advantages for the balance of payments, industrial efficiency, and investment, but all these would be negated if domestic prices rose leading to wage demands and cost increases. (The experience of price increases in countries adopting the VAT is discussed in chapter 10.)

8. The value added tax replacing other taxes: excises, the selective employment tax, income tax, and social security

General

The VAT need not necessarily replace only sales taxes or corporate income taxes. These are, admittedly, the obvious tax substitutions, but many others have been mooted, particularly the SET and some excises. Theoretically, the VAT could replace any tax. For instance, the *only* tax in the country could be a VAT. In a closed economy with no saving 'there is an equivalence between a personal income tax and the general sales tax. Similarly, there exists an equivalence between a general tax on the factor payments of firms and a spending tax on households. In other words, there exists an equivalence between all four types of truly general tax'.[1] Of course, these propositions have to be qualified as the highly artificial setting of assumptions is abandoned. So that when we talk about incidence allowing for capital formation, the statement becomes 'replacement of the income tax by a sales tax on consumers is to the disadvantage of consumers and the advantage of savers'.[2] Certainly, the VAT can be thought of as replacing any tax; the more complicated or distant the relationship of the tax being replaced by the VAT, the more likely it is that broad fiscal corrections in a number of taxes and government transfers will be necessary to offset inequities from the substitution. For instance, as mentioned under the discussion of various alternative rates of tax, the inherently regressive nature of a general sales tax can be offset by transfers to low income households. Indeed, it is probably more accurate and equitable to redistribute directly to households than to rely on highly discriminatory taxation of particular goods and services by multi-rate sales taxes.

[1] Musgrave, R. A: *Public Finance*, op. cit., p. 353.
[2] Ibid., p. 377.

Provided an open mind is kept on the opportunities and desirability of offsetting transfers to compensate low income families for price changes subsequent to the imposition of VAT, any tax could be replaced. However, even with transfers to compensate for regressiveness, the other effects of any given transfer may affect relative prices, distribution of income and wealth, incentives, efficiency, savings, and the balance of payments.

There are three main optional substitutions which are mentioned and which might be practical, these are:

    (a) Excises.
    (b) The SET and the regional employment premium.
    (c) Income tax and social security.

Excises

There are three main points relating to the VAT and excises. First, some excises enter into the costs of production and are not rebated on exports. These are a source of discriminatory taxation which affects free competition between countries. Second, excises are levied at very different rates in each European country and when the VAT is introduced on top of these high excises, it can lead to extraordinarily high rates of product taxation. Finally, for the EEC to achieve its avowed target of establishing all sales taxes on a country-of-origin principle, all sales tax systems, structures, and rates will have to be harmonized.

There is a single solution to all these difficulties, that is the harmonization of excise rates. Moreover, when excise rates are harmonized throughout the Community, this can mean reduced revenue to some countries. In turn, this can be made good by a higher VAT rate. In this way, the VAT is, if you like, substituted for the excise.

The main excise entering into the cost of production is that on hydrocarbon oils. All businesses pay this duty for transport, heating, power, plant, etc. The CBI estimates that about 60% of the hydrocarbon oil duty is paid in Britain by industry, i.e., £800 million in 1970 to '71. Similarly, Belgian industry welcomed the VAT because it gave a better chance of including all the fiscal 'upstream' charges. It is impossible to know how much duty has been paid in this way for any particular product. It may be different for each firm, and indeed between different plants within a firm, producing the same product, as the tax paid can vary depending on location, climate, efficiency, etc. With very different rates in each country, inequity is compounded. Clearly, the fairest way of ensuring equal competition between countries within a customs union would be to abolish such an excise and transfer the revenue burden to the VAT. All the tax could then be reclaimed on exported goods. In practice, this is impossible because excises are such an important revenue tax contributing from 13% of total consumption taxes in Belgium up to 24% of such taxes in Italy. They represent from 3·5% of total taxes in the Netherlands to 8% of total taxes in Italy. As the EEC Commission states: 'When we take the importance of the revenue brought into the states by these products (alcohol, petroleum, and tobacco) into account, it is obvious that it will be impossible to abolish the taxes concerned, but that they will have to be harmonized.'[3] Where these taxes already form a particularly important part of exchequer revenue (as they do in Britain, where hydrocarbon oils are approximately 7% of total taxation, tobacco 9%, and alcohol 6%), other existing sales taxes are levied at lower rates. The introduction of a VAT at a rate close to the 'normal' rate on the Continent of 15% would yield revenue substantially in excess of, for example, British purchase tax and SET (roughly £1630 million in excess). As excises on tobacco, alcohol, and oil amount to about £3450 million, this excess revenue would facilitate substantial reductions of excises equivalent to about 50% across the board.

Table 8.1
Approximate sales tax content of spirits, beer, cigarettes, and petrol in seven countries 1965/7

	UK	Ger-many	Italy	France	Bel-gium	Nether-lands	Ireland
Spirits (per gall)	14·60	5·12	3·10	3·10	6·19	5·34	13·27
Beer (per 36 galls)	8·55	1·72	4·32		1·05	0·53	18·00
Cigarettes*	80%	n.a.	n.a.	n.a.	58%	57%	77%
Petrol (gall)	0·16	0·11	0·24	0·21	0·11	0·11	0·19

* It should be noted that cigars are much more widely smoked on the Continent than in the UK, and *their* tax rate is only 12% in the Netherlands and Belgium, and 19% in Germany.

Source: Annual Report of the Revenue Commissioners 1966/67 and Dosser, D. and Han, S. S: *Taxes in the E.E.C. and Britain*, PEP, London, 1968, Table III, p. 13.

Rates of excise tax in the EEC are usually lower than in Britain. In Germany, for instance, the excise on spirits is one-third that in Britain while in France it is one-quarter, so that a reduction of over half would be needed to bring the British rates of excise on spirits into line. One the other hand, British excise on petrol is more likely to be about the average adopted by the EEC, as France and Italy have petrol excises at higher rates than those in Britain, but the rates in Germany and Italy are lower.

Clearly, if the higher yield of a broad based VAT were used to reduce the weight of excises, there would be substantial changes in relative prices. Consumer durables, cars, electrical appliances, etc., at present heavily

[3] Council of the EEC: Second Directive, 'On the Forms and Methods of Application of the Common System of Taxation on Value-Added', *Journal Officiel des Communautes Europeenes*, No. 71, 14 April 1967, p. 5.

taxed under the purchase tax structure, would have their tax liability reduced. Alcohol and tobacco would likewise have a lower tax liability. To compensate for these reductions, taxes would rise on clothing, housing, food, fuel, light, travel, books, entertainment, and many households goods. Merely to list those items which would bear a heavier tax emphasizes the quite different attitude to sales taxation on the Continent compared to that in Britain and Ireland.

Sales taxes in the British Isles are used deliberately as discriminatory taxes implying social (and moral) values. On the Continent, taxation is not used so obviously to sway consumer choice. Instead, the social security transfers correct the regressive nature of general broad based sales taxes and leave households free to vary their consumption pattern without the influence on relative prices of such extreme differential taxes as those in Britain.

Excises in particular are odd taxes. Those on alcohol and tobacco are undoubtedly regressive so that 'it would be possible to abolish the whole of Britain's taxes (other than surtaxes, death duties, and company taxation) and replace them by a uniform sales tax at around 28% and, if anything, leave the lower income group rather better than they are under our present tax system'.[4]

The excise on petrol, although not regressive, is nevertheless the most blatant example of a heavy tax entering into business costs and irrecoverable on exports. The British export rebate of 2% was justified by claiming that this 2% represented the spillover of hydrocarbon duty into export prices. A substitution of the VAT for the hydrocarbon excise would 'significantly relieve industrial costs and exports from indirect taxation'.[5]

So that for each excise, a good case either on the ground of its regressiveness, or the non-recovery on exports, can be made for its (at least partial) replacement by the VAT. In practice, any such change would be slow and probably only initiated under pressure from the EEC Commission. The ingrained determination of British puritanism to make pleasure expensive is unlikely to be quickly eroded by Continental habits.

The most likely policy for Britain and Ireland is to introduce the VAT, but ensure that it is not levied on top of existing excise rates; rather the excise rates should be reduced so that the combined excise and VAT would not alter the final total tax liability of the good at present bearing the excise. This was the practice in the Netherlands when the rates of tax on tobacco, alcohol, and cars were adjusted 'to keep the rates at which these items are taxed at approximately the same levels as those which obtained under the former turnover tax'.[6] The same procedure was adopted with German excises. Scandinavian countries have been tougher in their treatment of goods already

---

[4] Merrett and Monk: *Bulletin of the Oxford Institute of Economics and Statistics*, August 1966.
[5] NEDO: *Value Added Tax*, op. cit., para. 5.71.
[6] Ibid., para. 4.46.

heavily taxed by excises; Denmark and Sweden both superimposed a single-rate VAT on top of already high excises. But this was possible because of a highly developed system of government transfer payments, and in the case of Denmark, a simultaneous substantial revision of the total tax structure.

After the tax substitution, as the harmonization of excise rates in the Community is carried out, almost certainly the rates of excise on tobacco and alcohol in Britain will be reduced and that on petrol might well be unchanged as other countries approximated to the British rate.

This sort of revision would be unlikely to affect savings or incentives as essentially it is a change between different forms of sales taxes. But the change in relative prices might well alter consumer preferences; services would be taxed at higher rates than at present and demand for them might grow more slowly, but the lower excises on alcohol and tobacco could lead to an increased demand for those products. Even if their excises were not reduced absolutely, their excise burden would be reduced relative to, for example, clothing, and this could increase the quantity demanded. The effect of such excise changes on exports would not necessarily be as favourable as many think. To take an extreme example, if all the duty on hydrocarbon oils were transferred to a VAT and rebated on exports, this would reduce the tax base and from this reduced domestic tax base an equivalent yield must be obtained which, in turn, means a higher tax rate on domestic sales. This higher tax rate could induce wage claims which would erode the export price advantage. All in all, the most attractive feature of substituting the VAT for part of present excises is the reduction of the influence of taxation on relative prices and consumer choice. But this requires dependent assumptions on the rates at which the VAT is introduced, and on transfers to lower income households. This attractive feature is precisely that which, as revealed by past and current fiscal decisions, British governments do not favour. They view taxation as a discriminatory device deliberately designed to influence consumer choice. It will probably take a long time to move them from this view point. Nevertheless move they must. The EEC seems determined to press ahead with the implementation of changes in all sales taxes so that the whole Community can change over to a country-of-origin principle rather than the present country-of-destination principle. Excises within the Community vary enormously both in the goods they apply to and in the rates at which they are applied. There appears to be agreement on a common range of excises, tobacco, spirits, beer, hydrocarbon oils, and possibly wine and sugar. Countries that levy excises on other goods will have to phase them out.

With the certainty of excise and VAT harmonization, there will be considerable changes in British consumption patterns.

The SET and the regional employment premium

The SET is a poll tax on each person employed in the service industries. As such, it raises the cost of services not only to the general public but also to industry. Thus an industry's costs are raised according to the amount of service inputs it buys.

The increased costs resulting from the SET are, like petrol excises, irrecoverable on goods exported. Depending on the mix of exports and their respective inputs of taxed services, part of the revenue raised by the SET increases export prices. The removal of the SET and the substitution of a VAT will allow recovery of this tax element in exports. Again, to the extent that it is recovered, the tax revenue to the exchequer will be reduced and if an equal yield is required from the substitution, the tax rate on domestic sales will have to be raised. The increase in domestic prices could lead to wage demands and further cost increases to industry which would enter into export prices and which could vitiate the advantage of the recovery of VAT (replacing SET) on exports.

Table 8.2
Service inputs to selected industries

	Services £ million	Services as percentage of total purchases of goods and services
Agriculture	250	25
Oil refining	67	16
Other chemical	331	30
Metal manufacturing	255	28
Engineering	816	25
Textiles	159	20

Source: *National Income and Expenditure 1966, HMSO, 1966, Table 19, p. 24. Summary input–output transactions matrix 1963.*

In its original form, the SET was designed to provide an export subsidy to manufactured goods. The tax comprised not only a poll tax on services but a rebate of the tax paid and a premium on top of that to manufacturers. In this way industry, which was assumed to have a greater capacity for productivity increases than service industries and which would therefore improve the balance of payments, obtained a subsidy but did not directly contravene the GATT regulations. This relative subsidy to manufacturers has been abolished except for those industries situated in the Development Areas where the subsidy is now known as the regional employment premium.

As this subsidy is no longer directly linked to the SET, its replacement by the VAT would not necessarily involve the abolition of the regional employment premium. The regional employment premium would be considered seperately under the Community decisions on regional policy and could certainly exist side by side with a VAT.

Apart from its effect on export prices, the SET also affects the relative weights of tax between services and goods. It affects productivity in the distributive trade and in manufacturing. It also creates interesting problems of definition. These points will be considered below in relation to the VAT substitution.

One of the main reasons given for introducing the SET in July 1966 was that goods were heavily taxed whereas services were not. As the Chancellor said in his budget speech:

> The value of the manufactured goods subject to purchase tax and excise duties which consumers at present buy, comes to about £6000 million excluding the cost of distribution. Out of this sum, tax accounts for about 40%. But the sum which consumers pay for services of various kinds including the distribution of the goods they buy but excluding passenger transport is even larger . . . about £7000 million. And out of this sum indirect tax accounts for less than 1%.

In this way, consumer choice was skewed and demand for services artificially stimulated. The SET was seen as going some way (but by no means all the way) towards closing this tax gap between goods and services.

The VAT does not discriminate at all. Indeed its so-called 'neutrality' is often quoted by Continental writers as its main advantage. As such, it would tax most services in the same way it taxes goods. Unless it was decided that services should be *penalized* relative to goods by a special tax like the SET, the SET would be rendered superfluous by the introduction of the VAT.

Roughly, the present SET, as a percentage on consumer expenditure on services, represents a tax of 9% on services. A VAT at the 'normal' rate of, say, 15% would represent a 6% increase in the tax burden of services.

This raises the interesting point that, in contrast to excises, the SET is probably progressive according to income. As income rises, households and individuals tend to spend an increasing proportion of their income on services. Thus a substitution of the VAT for the SET which also raised the tax burden on services could also be progressive.

Table 6.1, page 80, showed the SET allocated to consumer expenditure by the Central Statistics Office (column 3). If it is assumed that in any substitution of the VAT for the SET, the yield on public authority sales and intermediate sales is not replaced, but that the yield of SET on present export sales and on gross domestic capital formation will be replaced (because of the complete offset for these items in the VAT), then the net yield of the SET which needs to be replaced is approximately £500 million. If this is added to the required replacement yield of the purchase tax discussed in chapter 6, £1000 million, the total required yield of the two taxes when replaced by the VAT is £1500 million.

Table 6.1, column 8, shows the sort of yield which might be expected from a VAT replacing the purchase tax and SET at rates of 10% and 20% (which are not so very different from many of the rates at present in force in many of the EEC countries). The yield is just over £1500 million and should represent a reasonable replacement. As before, food, alcohol, and housing are exempted. Because of the higher VAT rates used, it is also possible to exempt fuel and light and clothing and footwear from the tax base. The high rate of 20% is levied on motor cars and motor cycles, furniture and floor coverings, radio, electrical, and other durables, textiles, soft furnishings, chemists goods, miscellaneous recreational goods, and other miscellaneous goods. The prices of most of these items, compared to the present taxes, could be expected to rise; an enormous weight is thrown on the assumed 10% VAT on the running costs of vehicles. To the extent that this proved impossible, the tax would have to be redistributed under other items. However, what the rough outline in Table 6.1 shows is that it is perfectly practicable to replace the purchase tax and SET using a VAT at two rates, 10% and 20%, and yet still having very substantial exemptions to ensure that the tax is not strikingly regressive.

There is one further financial difficulty about such substitution. Part of the SET revenue represents an interest free forced 'loan' by industry to the government. Manufacturers who are exempt must first pay the tax before it is eventually refunded to them some six months later. Probably the best way to treat this once and for all charge on the transition from SET to VAT is by borrowing.

The SET also affects productivity. As a head tax on labour, the cost of labour inputs is raised relative to capital. This should encourage taxed services to economize on staff. The Reddaway Report indicated that the gain in productivity (in the distributive trades) over and above expected productivity in the period 1966 to 1968 (inclusive) was between 1·7% and 5·8%. 'The saving in payroll costs through higher productivity went a long way towards offsetting the cost of the SET.'[7] If the SET was replaced by a VAT, would this incentive be removed and the trend towards greater producitivty reversed?

The removal of the SET would be unlikely actually to reverse the trend. It might reduce the incentive a little, or it might be that this increase in productivity was some once and for all slack available to be taken up in these trades. More likely, however, is that the SET simply reinforced an already existing trend towards more automated services and this would be likely to continue, especially as the VAT replacing the SET might be at a higher rate.

The VAT would, if absorbed and levied at a rate approximating closely to the Continental 'normal' rates, raise taxation on wages and profits in the services compared to the SET. This might encourage even more productivity. Of course, if both the SET and the VAT are passed on, the change is seen in relative prices. However, the Reddaway Report indicated

[7] Reddaway, W. B: *Effect of the Selective Employment Tax, First Report, the Distributive Trades*, HMSO, London, 1970, p. 208.

that at least some of the SET was absorbed and, therefore, it might be assumed that part of the VAT would also be seen as a tax on wages and profits.

More important than the debate in the First Report of the Reddaway Commission are the disincentives of the SET to productivity in manufacturing. The original SET contained a positive inducement to use labour rather than capital as the rebate was paid as a head subsidy. This actually encouraged labour intensive methods of production. This, happily, has been removed, but a more subtle influence remains.

The definition of a manufacturing plant not liable to SET, as opposed to a service plant which is liable, revolves round the employment of the majority of workers. If the majority are designated as manufacturing workers then *all the workers* in the plant escape SET liability. In this way, if 51 workers in a plant of 100 are defined as manufacturers, the plant pays no SET. If 3 of those workers leave due to increased manufacturing productivity, there is then a majority (49 to 48) of the workers designated as service employees and the *entire* plant switches and becomes liable to the SET. So that at the margin, the incentive to employ unnecessary manufacturing labour can be extremely high. The replacement of the SET by the VAT would remove this extraordinary anomaly.

From this anomaly stems the final problem of definition under the SET structure. In determining whether the majority of workers are or are not employed in the provision of services, an important definition is that of the 'plant' or employment unit. This cannot be a whole company which might have numerous offices and factories spread throughout the country, and yet the problem of a cohesive definition at factory or plant level is also difficult. The solution adopted was to select as a single plant an area not divided by a public road. This means that if a public road happens to divide the offices and transport sections of a factory from the manufacturing section, then the SET is levied on one part of the factory but not on the other. In evidence to the NEDO, it was pointed out that 'the SET leads to gross anomalies in the siting of offices, computers, warehouses, and decisions on staffing'.[8]

The VAT would have no such quixotic effects and by its blanket coverage would encourage industry to site its production facilities according to industrial sense rather than for tax considerations.

It is reasonable to accept that some taxes should be designed to influence industrial decisions, say, for regional policy, but the important word is 'designed'. If taxes encourage businesses or individuals to act in peculiar and odd ways purely to minimize tax liability and not to fulfil any social and/ or economic end, then the tax is suspect. It is the unfortunate distinction of the SET that, although having some desirable effects, it also creates many quirks and oddities which reduce its usefulness. The VAT could replace the

[8] NEDO: *Value Added Tax*, op. cit., A.76.

SET and if some aspects of the SET were thought worth retaining, they could be achieved in other ways.

For instance, if a penalty on employment in services relative to employment in other productive activities was thought desirable, then a payroll tax (linked to social security contributions) could be levied on designated service employees. Admittedly this would probably be unfortunate as it raises all those questions of a *taxe opaque* in exports mentioned earlier, but it could be done.

Income tax and social security

Income tax and social security are taken together as constituting a range from positive to negative taxation. When the VAT is introduced, a basic decision must be whether to attempt rough and ready progression by using multiple rates (see chapter 5) or to levy a single rate and compensate low income households in other ways for any increase in the cost of living.

When the VAT is substituted for other sales taxes like the purchase tax and excises, the political temptation is to try to minimize price changes arising from the substitution. To do this, rates of VAT are adopted which closely parallel existing rates. In this way, hopefully, prices are unchanged and real incomes are unchanged, and presumably political hot potatoes do not have to be handled or eaten. But it does lead to the messy system of multiple rates, numerous exemptions, and expensive administration. It is reckoned that a two-rate system of VAT costs 80% more to administer than a single-rate system.[9] For instance, if the VAT were introduced in Britain as she entered the EEC, it could be argued politically inexpedient to apply it to food, except confectionery, ice-cream, and soft drinks which are already liable to purchase tax. The argument would be that it would be particularly awkward to levy a tax on food at a time when food prices would be rising because of a movement towards import levies and away from food subsidies.

The alternative is administratively and socially more attractive, but often difficult and awkward to 'sell'. A single-rate VAT would be cheap to administer, it also involves numerous changes in relative prices and is probably regressive. But reductions in income tax could compensate families who paid income tax but would not affect those who were not taxpayers. Adjustments would have to be made by transfer payments to low income households, and this would give an opportunity for a substantial overhaul of social security payments.

As one of the aims of the EEC is harmonization of the social security system, the substitution of the VAT could provide a useful catalyst to begin a reform of social security in Britain and Ireland towards the pattern in the EEC. As Table 8.3 shows, the structures of employers' social security payments in the EEC and those of Britain and Ireland are very different.

[9] Rybczynski T. M., Ed: *The Value Added Tax*, op. cit., p. 9.

Table 8.3
Social security contributions in Europe

Country	Social security contributions as a percentage of GNP at factor cost	Employers contributions to social security as a percentage of	
		total taxation	GNP at factor cost
France	17·1	26·8	11·9
Belgium	10·1	21·3	6·7
Germany	11·7	15·3	5·9
Norway	—	11·1	4·3
Sweden	—	9·0	3·8
UK	5·5	7·2	2·4
Ireland	1·1	3·4	1·0

Source: OECD, Border Tax Adjustments and Tax Structures, Paris, 1968, p. 198–200.

Of course, such a tax substitution involving not only the introduction of the new VAT and the abolition of familiar taxes, but also considerable changes in taxes and transfers not directly related to the sales tax change, creates large political problems. It may be politically more expedient to take several bites at the cherry. The first bite would be the VAT substitution with as few changes in relative prices as possible. Rationalization towards a single-rate VAT might follow a few years later along with gradual changes in transfer payments and income taxes.

As stated earlier, Denmark was the only country to use the introduction of the VAT as an opportunity for a major restructuring of taxation. A system of PAYE was introduced at the same time as the VAT, as well as changes in the rates of income tax, personal allowances, and transfers. It is worth noting that Denmark combined these changes with a straightforward single-rate VAT which greatly simplified the administration and resulted in a very low collection cost.

Other countries which have shown an interest in using the VAT as a partial replacement for income tax have been those with extensive social security systems. So that Sweden and Norway both have high wages, high income taxes, and comprehensive social security structures, and both are concerned to use the VAT at least to stop further increases in income taxation and probably to reduce such taxation.

Minimum requirements for any replacement of income tax by VAT would be the existence of efficient, wide ranging, social services and a willingness on the government's part to use them to compensate low income families for regressive changes in relative prices.

A final comment on possible substitution uses for the VAT is the report that the US is considering a VAT to raise money to pay for the scheme (long postponed) of sharing Federal revenues with the individual States. The attraction of a VAT for this purpose lies in its (possibly misplaced) reputation as a large money raiser. The preference for a VAT has been reinforced by the report of a 'task force' on business taxation appointed by the President in September 1969. In its report it did not recommend a VAT as a substitute for the corporation income tax or for social security payroll taxes, but it did say that if future revenue requirements exceeded the yield of existing taxes, then the additional revenue should be found by indirect taxes rather than direct, and the tax favoured would be either a VAT or a single-stage sales tax at the Federal level.

Summary

    (a) Substitution of the VAT for excises would reduce present regressiveness of sales taxes and would reduce the influence of taxation on relative prices and consumer choice.

    (b) The EEC determination to harmonize sales tax rates and coverage implies substantial changes in British consumption patterns.

    (c) The VAT could replace the SET and still leave the regional employment premium.

    (d) The removal of the SET and the substitution of the VAT is unlikely to affect productivity adversely.

    (e) When the VAT replaces the SET many of the anomalies in the siting of offices, computers, and service facilities, and inefficient staffing will be removed.

    (f) To replace income tax (in part) by the VAT requires offsetting adjustments in social services, which in turn require an efficient and wide range of such services.

    (g) The US is reported to be considering a Federal VAT to finance the sharing of Federal revenue with States.

9. Administration, statistical information, evasion, fiscal policy, and regional policy

Administrative arguments

Many of the main administrative arguments in favour of using the VAT do not apply, or apply less appropriately, to Britain at the moment than to the other countries in Europe when they adopted the VAT. The four main arguments can be itemized:

(a) **Knowing the VAT content.** Under the VAT it is possible to know the tax content of a product at any stage of production. This is particularly important when goods are exported and the full tax content is to be reclaimed, or when goods are imported and a completely equivalent tax is to be imposed. The importance of this is clear in a customs union where a fundamental requisite of the economic union is competition on an equal basis. While Britain is not in the EEC and can take unilateral action deliberately to penalize imports, e.g., the special levy, then to know the exact tax content of her exports is not so important.

Of course, the present British wholesale tax is easily deducted from exports or, indeed, imposed on imports. Nevertheless, it is true that British exports do include some wholesale tax which is not deductable.

(b) **Neutrality of the VAT.** It is claimed that the VAT is neutral in that it does not distort, or favour, any particular method of production. This is also probably true of general wholesale and retail sales taxes.

It is also claimed that the VAT, because it is spread evenly throughout the production chain, does not cause undue strain at any point. Wholesale or retail sales taxes are contrasted to this because they fall on a single link in the production chain, and this link is often held to be the weakest in the chain. Weakest in the sense that the firms liable to tax are often small, poorly equipped to deal with the taxes, and difficult to check.

Is this true? The wholesale and retail sales taxes in Britain have proved extremely successful. They are accepted and familiar and yet are administratively cheap and have not created an insupportable administrative load on the shops and wholesalers dealing with the tax.

Very often the argument about the weakest link is used by countries that have never tried such taxes, whose civil service is unused to this type of tax, and whose public regard it suspiciously. Where single-stage sales taxes have proved successful, as in Britain, such an argument cannot be accepted.

Yet one of the more persuasive administrative arguments for introducing a VAT into Britain is that high rates of sales taxes falling on one or two stages might create taxpayer resistance which would result in administrative problems and evasions (see below for a more detailed comment on evasion). The highest rate of British purchase tax (55%) is a super luxury rate by European standards. If it is necessary to increase the yields of sales taxes to such a level, then there might be administrative gains in spreading the tax liability over all stages of production. Nevertheless, it should be emphasized that spreading the load does not alter the burden; any gain to taxpayers is largely psychological.

(c) Unavoidability of the VAT. A retail sales tax can be avoided by out-of-state purchases. It is claimed that the VAT cannot be avoided in the same way. In the US a major problem of sales taxes is the easy avoidance of a State's high sales taxes by persons who purchase their goods across the State boundary in a neighbouring State with a lower rate, or sometimes with no sales taxes at all. In this way, the original State loses all sales tax revenue.

If the EEC countries had adopted a retail sales tax with different rates in each country, then similar avoidance might have happened. Under the VAT, operated on the destination principle (all taxable products having the same destination or subjected to the same tax burden which is the form used at present in the EEC), much the same problem arises. Exports are free of tax, and if taxed under the VAT at a lower rate in a neighbouring state, can be bought easily and cheaply by the nationals of the original exporting state. It is true, that when the good is reimported, then the tax liability at the border can easily be computed under the indirect subtracted VAT; but this is equally true with the retail sales tax. Of course, it is almost impossible to catch and tax services consumed or rendered outside the state, or indeed some purchases of goods, e.g., subscriptions to magazines. But this, once more, is true of both single-stage sales taxes and multi-stage taxes.

In general, there does not seem to be much to choose between a well administered single-stage tax and a VAT in terms of out-of-state purchases made to evade tax.

(d) The major European sales tax. We are left with one other administrative advantage of the VAT. It is the main sales tax in Europe. When trading with European countries using the VAT, the tax content of sales and purchases is known, and the competitive position is clear. If Britain enters the EEC, she will have to adopt the VAT. It might be reasonable to argue that Britain should move herself voluntarily towards the sales tax structure which has been accepted by most countries in Europe.

In this case, discussion as to whether this move is administratively easy or not, pales into insignificance. It becomes a political and economic commitment to a European, rather than a British, structure of sales taxes.

Costs of administration

Compared to existing British sales taxes, the administration of a VAT is likely to be more complicated and expensive. Sales taxation in Britain is different to that which existed in the countries which formed the original EEC. These countries all used sales taxes which, in one way or another, involved taxing each stage of production. In France, it was the first simple form of VAT; in Germany, it was a cascade tax on turnovers. But in each case the substitution of the VAT did not involve, for the original members of the EEC, a very substantial increase in the number of taxpayers, except where the retail stage had been exempt previously and the new tax base was extended to include this stage. (See Table 9.1.) The retail stage had been exempt in both Denmark and the Netherlands.

Table 9.1 clearly shows how the Scandinavian countries Denmark, Norway, and Sweden which had single-stage taxes, suffered under the transition to the VAT. The number of taxpayers in Denmark increased eight times, in Norway trebled, and in Sweden doubled. In the Netherlands, taxpayers under the previous system were approximately three-quarters of those under the present VAT system. This increase is mainly accounted for by the extension of the tax to the retail stage. In France, where the tax was extended to include the retail stage, the increase in taxpayers was not so great because retailers, although not taxed under the VAT system, were liable previously to special local taxes. Germany actually had a small reduction in the number of taxpayers liable under the new tax.

In Britain, a changeover to the VAT would involve an extension of the tax base and an influx of new taxpayers who are at present not liable to tax under the wholesale taxes. The number of transactions covered by the Revenue Commissioners would expand from 65000 to 2 million. To administer the VAT on the EEC indirect subtractive base including the retail stage, and to substitute this for the purchase tax, would need an additional staff of 8000.[1] If the VAT was only imposed up to and including the wholesale stage, the extra staff needed would be about 7000. Even if the most economical (in terms of staffing) system of VAT were used, by assessing the tax liability from annual accounts (the additive method), some 4000 to 5000 more staff would still be needed.

[1] NEDO: *Value Added Tax*, op. cit., para. 5.26.

Table 9.1

Taxpayers and officials under the VAT system and other previous systems

	France	Germany	Netherlands	Denmark	Norway	Sweden
(a) Taxpayers under the previous system as a percentage of taxpayers under the VAT system	86	103	73	13	32	51
(b) Taxpayers under VAT as a percentage of the population	4·1	2·7	2·8	7·5	7·3	4·6
(c) Taxpayers per tax official	255	—	298	—	350	596
(d) Tax officials, old system, as a percentage of officials under the new system	84	100	75	100	75	49

It is true that staff released from dealing with purchase tax and SET would be available for transfer. It is worth noting that there is little to be saved in administrative expenses if the VAT only partially replaces other taxes rather than completely replaces them. A tax abolished dispenses with its full apparatus and the administrators are freed for other work. A reduction in a tax rate, e.g., excises, income tax, profits tax, does little to alter the administrative burden of running the tax. The greatest administrative saving, therefore, comes from complete tax substitution.

It is clear that the administrative costs of a VAT in Britain would be high. One figure given is £16 million.[2] Much would depend, however, on the co-operation received from businesses, and the requirements of control, verification, and appeals. In turn, the co-operation of businesses might depend on the exact form of the tax. A multi-rate VAT requires more elaborate and time consuming completion of tax returns than does a single rate. The French tax form appears complicated because of the different rates and exemptions. If you insist on including with the VAT collection, the tax on behalf of the 'professional committee for horology' at 0·70%, or the 'contribution to the dying and technical centre' at 1%, then clearly the tax return will be complicated. The more complicated the return, the less co-operative the businessman is likely to be.

The least complicated VAT is levied at a single rate. The Danes manage to get tax returns of their single-rate VAT on to a postcard. As a result, though taxpayers increased eightfold, there was no increase in the officials needed to run the new tax. (See Table 9.1.) It cannot be emphasized too often that the least complicated VAT is a single-rate tax with very few exemptions or special provisions. Some indication of the relative efficiency of the tax administrations is given in Table 9.1 where the Swedish official deals with 596 taxpayers while his French opposite number can cope only with under half that number (255).

An example of the sort of difficulties awkward provisions can make comes from the treatment of expenses in Germany. Expenses paid to staff in Germany can be claimed as a VAT credit for the tax content they contain, but the State lays down the allowable percentages. Thus, 11% of hotel costs are attributed to the VAT, railway tickets and taxis up to 50 kilometres distance are allowed at 5·5%, journeys over 50 kilometres are allowed at 11%, and the use of a car is allowed at 11% on a base of 90% of the car allowance.[3] Clearly, a single rate with as few exceptions as possible reduces the cost of such returns to the business.

The cost to business of administering the new tax would be greatest in the initial years when new procedures would have to be adopted and possibly new clerical staff employed, or existing staff retrained. Although large computerized firms in Germany found their extra expenses to be nil, smaller

[2] NEDO: *Value Added Tax*, op. cit., para. 5.26.
[3] Rybczynski T. M., Ed: op. cit., p. 41.

businesses estimated their costs had risen by up to 20%. At the same time, it is probably true that the collection of data, on a monthly or quarterly basis, in a form to be used for the VAT, is the sort of information an efficient firm ought to have in any case. The new tax might be thought of as a means of prodding inefficient businesses into doing what they ought to be doing.

An extension of this though is that the introduction of the VAT is often accompanied by a minor boom in simple calculating machines—once more probably a desirable development. But there is also the cost to businesses which must rewrite computer programmes to ensure that VAT credit is claimed on all purchases and that all sales show VAT liability. About ten months to a year has proved adequate time for these company adjustments.

An efficient means of collection was devised in Germany where there are three parts to the collection system:

(a) A monthly *self assessment* of tax liability, and the tax paid to the local authorities (Lander).
(b) Verification and control by *spot checks* on purchase invoices (which could be computerized, see below) at yearly to five yearly intervals.
(c) Annual verification, by the auditors, on the basis of the *company account* for profits tax liability.

This leaves the business to conduct its own assessments which the auditors can verify as part of their normal routine on profits tax computation. The only direct contact with the state arises when a spot check verification is carried out, which for large firms is likely to be annually and for small ones to be as infrequent as once in every five years.

Visits to traders are conducted very differently by each country. France, Germany, and the Netherlands reckon to visit a trader on average every four years. This can vary considerably, however, depending on the size of the firm, e.g., in France small traders have, in the past, been visited only every 23 years. Denmark and Luxembourg carry out visits every 3 years.

The system should be as simple as possible, for instance, there is no need to require export refund claims to be accompanied by copies of the shipping bills. These can simply be held by the firm and be vouched for on audit. Probably a good system is that in Sweden where there are random spot checks and verifications from income tax returns.

The costs of administration in a small country where multi-stage industrial linkages are few are not likely to be as important as in a highly industrialized country like Britain or Germany.

Finally, whether in a large or small country, the means of payment should be as simple as possible. Denmark and Sweden oblige firms to make payments through the postal Giro system. This is efficient. It is also a way of guaranteeing a considerable volume of business for the state Giro system.

An ingenious method of VAT collection and administration is suggested by Professor Wheatcroft in the context of administering an account type of VAT, but it is applicable to other forms.[4] The idea revolves round the creation of special bank accounts by firms, into which they pay all money receipts for taxable goods and services and from which they make all payments for taxable goods and services. If the VAT rate was say 15%, when the account is cleared (at any time) 15% of the account is transferred to the revenue authorities and the remainder to the non-tax account of the taxpayer. At any given time, if the tax account were in debit, either the debit could be carried forward or the account could be cleared by a transfer of funds from the revenue authorities. This is a fascinating scheme which deserves wider discussion than it has received since its publication.

Frequency of collection and invoicing

Clearly the costs of collection are less the more infrequently the tax is levied. A quarterly tax could still be efficient and much less trouble than a monthly one. The EEC Commission suggests in article 12 (3) of the Second Directive that any taxable person must file a declaration (showing tax liability on sales and tax credits on purchases) each month. The tax is paid on filing the declaration. 'The monthly period may, however, for practical reasons, be shortened or lengthened and certain persons may be authorized to file declarations each quarter, half year, or year.'[5] Each country has its own particular system for dealing with the taxable period. In France, taxpayers can select one of two methods to declare their taxable sales; they can submit their return before the twenty-fifth day of the month which follows that month for which the sales are assessed, and the tax is then paid at the same time. Instead, they may opt to make fixed monthly payments of an amount agreed with the revenue. The amount cannot be less than one-twelfth of the tax paid in the previous year. When this method is used, a full return for the year must be submitted before 1 February of the following year and any balance of VAT paid before 25 April of that year. Very small traders can submit returns every three months.

In Germany, the tax must be paid within ten days of the end of each taxable period, and this is usually one month. Very small traders can submit their returns every three months.

In the Netherlands, the taxable period is three months. The VAT becomes payable in the month which follows the end of the three-month taxable period. Taxpayers can, if they wish, opt for a one-month taxable period or the authorities can insist that the taxpayer adopt a monthly return.

In Belgium, the taxable period is one month and at the end the taxpayer makes a self-assessment of the amount of VAT liability. A check is carried

[4] Wheatcroft, G. S. A.: 'Some Administrative Problems of an Added Value Tax', *British Tax Review*, September/October 1963, p. 349–352.

[5] International Bureau of Fiscal Documentation: *European Taxation*, Vol. 7, July/August 1967, p. 195.

out by an annual statement which must show the value of all sales and costs deducted; that is, the check is carried out using the additive method of calculation.

Sweden collects the tax every two months, and Denmark each quarter. The less frequent collection is a useful, flexible device which might be used more widely than at present.

The role played by invoices in the VAT structure is clearly crucial. Invoices have to be issued to consignees for all goods delivered and all taxable services performed by any enterprise which is registered for VAT. If, as sometimes happens, some payment is to be made for a partial delivery before the entire delivery has been completed, then separate invoices have to be made out for the parts which will eventually make up the whole. Of course, credit notes have to be issued for goods returned after an invoice has been issued.

The actual definition of 'delivery' is also crucial. Delivery is usually defined, when a product is transported, as taking place at the point where transportation begins. Obviously, at other times, where no carriage is involved, then delivery is located where the product is located.

Deliveries of goods and the rendering of services are taxable only when they are actually performed in the country where the VAT liability arises. If a good is imported, the delivery by the foreigner, by definition, takes place abroad (unless the goods happen to be imported without a designated buyer and a buyer is subsequently found). Considerable problems of definition and administration occur. For instance, a foreigner might sell goods in Britain, and as the delivery of the goods takes place abroad, British VAT is not liable on that particular sale. But if the foreigner has undertaken advertising, and has stayed in Britain to promote his sales, then he will have paid VAT on his advertising and hotel expenses. He should then be able to claim a refund of this VAT from the British revenue. However, this refund can only be paid if the hotel bill is in connection with a business trip; if the trip was in the nature of a holiday then no refund would be allowable. Clearly then, the distinction between business and holiday trips becomes very delicate.

One of the attractions of the VAT is the potential once and for all gain in revenue if it replaces a tax which is collected less frequently, e.g., profits tax. But the VAT ought also to yield a once and for all gain even if it replaces a monthly collective tax like the purchase tax. Because VAT is collected at all stages *before* the wholesale stage, many businesses will become liable to tax as soon as the VAT is introduced. Under a wholesale or retail sales tax, the goods produced by these earlier stages would only be liable to tax when they eventually got to the wholesale stage. Therefore, even if the VAT were levied at quarterly intervals, there could be a gain in revenue to the state compared to the monthly purchase tax This gain could be used to ease the main transitional difficulties for businesses.

Transitions

The transitional administrative costs could be high. In the Netherlands, an extensive campaign was mounted to educate everyone about the new VAT. Special television courses were arranged for retailers. Manuals and guides were printed for producers. Special visits were made to those who had to pay the VAT, including every retailer. Unusual transitional arrangements had to be made for inventories held at the moment the VAT was introduced.

Such costs would not be as high in Britain as on the Continent. The change from retail and wholesale taxes to a VAT is not as disruptive as changing from a cascade tax to a VAT. Moreover, most capital goods are not taxed in Britain and, therefore, their treatment presents little problem.

Stocks might be a transitional problem. If a business buys stocks before the VAT is introduced, the invoices for these goods will not show any VAT and, therefore, credit against VAT liability, once the tax has been introduced, cannot be claimed. The business must decide whether the prices of its stock purchases will be sufficiently low before the introduction of the VAT to offset the disadvantage of not being able to claim credit. The same reasoning must be applied to capital projects: should they be delayed until the new tax is operating or should they be implemented without delay?

This problem would be relatively trivial for British industry if the VAT was simply replacing present wholesale taxes. All stock held by businesses operating before the wholesale stage is tax free at present and, therefore, cheaper than it would be under the VAT. The calculation then becomes one of the cost of buying and keeping the stock compared to the likely price rise in stock purchases with the addition of the VAT. For businesses already liable to the wholesale taxes, the judgement depends on the new VAT rate compared to the present tax. If the new tax rate is higher, some stock piling will pay; though the government might be prepared to calculate purchase tax liability on stocks and reimburse companies. This would be a further complication. For instance, some German firms found that government repayments of previous tax paid on stocks more than compensated for the reduction in price from suppliers. Thus it paid the business to stock pile and claim from the government.

The calculations are much more complicated if the VAT is replacing other taxes. If the SET were replaced at the same time, clearly the prices of many goods would change depending on their designation as services or manufactures, and also depending on the amount of services they consumed. Happily, services cannot be stocked so at least that difficulty is removed.

If the VAT replaced profits or income taxes, and was combined with changes in social security systems, then it might pay businesses to overhaul the whole relationship of capital to labour (see chapters 7 and 8).

In Germany, the changeover, on 1 January 1968, caused many of these difficulties. The old cascade tax was levied on a price inclusive of the tax.

The VAT is levied on a price net of the tax. Therefore, the substitution involved important bargaining by businesses to obtain from their suppliers the best price possible. The key man in these negotiations was the firm's buyer of materials. 'The coming of the added value tax, was called "the buyers hour". The buyer had the job of inducing the supplier to pass on in his own prices the advantage which accrued to him through the elimination of his turnover tax and the cheapening of his purchases'.[6] If the seller of products in Germany was not obliged to reduce his prices by his customers and/or by competition, then he increased his profits. The trick lay in maximizing profits by squeezing your suppliers and in not being squeezed too much yourself.

Depending on the sort of substitution, British firms might have to take some very neat decisions. The purchase tax is calculated on a basis excluding the tax, as is the usual Continental VAT. Sales between registered firms are tax free, so no difficult problems arise in the straightforward substitution of the VAT for the purchase tax. Once other taxes are also reduced or abolished, the calculations of transitional policy become more complicated. If the VAT were substituted for excises, there might be some considerable transitional once and for all redistribution of tax burdens through industry. Under the system of bonded warehouses, excise has been liable as the good leaves the duty free zone. This places the immediate total burden of tax payment on the initial manufacturer. If the equivalent tax was fractionated through the industry, the present initial manufacturer would have a substantial reduction in tax financing while other later manufacturers would become liable to the VAT. Of course, these later processes would find their purchase prices of materials lower as the initial tax content has dropped. This is probably an area where the industry itself should negotiate for fair treatment and the government would probably be obliged to compensate firms for stocks of goods on which excise had already been paid.

For both industry and government, a new tax, like the VAT, especially one which replaces the well known taxes, would create uncertainty. It will require numerous decisions on tax liabilities, exemptions, and treatment. Unfamiliarity with the form of tax could hamper its introduction. In addition to the propaganda mentioned above, it might be sensible to appoint a board to have final administrative power to decide on:

(a) The extent of tax liability.
(b) The definition of taxable value.
(c) The scope of exemptions.
(d) Credit offsets.
(e) Appeals against assessments.
(f) Special transitional costs.
(g) Suggestions for amendment.

[6] Rybczynski, T. M., Ed: *The Value Added Tax*, op. cit., p. 36.

Such a board in Denmark, appointed by the Minister of Finance, is composed of 'eight members, two of whom (including the chairman) shall be judges and six shall possess general knowledge of administrative affairs and economic affairs'.[7] Such a board would be particularly useful during the transitional period.

Finally, the administrative costs of assessing, collecting, and verifying the VAT liability of small traders could be high. (See chapters 3 and 10.) It is reckoned that reasonable exemptions of such small businesses reduce the number of taxpayers by one-third. Whatever system is adopted, the definition of small businesses always creates problems. Business turnover can fluctuate. Sometimes a business can be above the maximum turnover for the definition of a small trader and ought to be classified as are other businesses; the next year it may be back below the crucial turnover figure. There is no simple answer to such businesses but it is clear that fairly flexible decisions in respect of them do pay off in lower administrative costs.

Statistical information

It is under this heading that some of the most weighty arguments in favour of a VAT arise. It is sometimes held that these advantages are all in the government's favour and that none helps the private sector. This is untrue, as will be shown. There are, at least, three main areas of statistical information where the VAT helps the private sector. But first, consider the processing of the tax.

On the *maximum information* VAT return, each taxpayer would submit monthly:

(a) His code number, which subsumes
    (i) a regional code number,
    (ii) an industrial classification number.

(b) His total purchases of goods and services on standard vouchers giving
    (i) suppliers code number,
    (ii) code numbers for current goods,
    (iii) code numbers for capital goods.

(c) Retailers would have to give total sales of goods and services, but code numbers need only give product type (even this is not absolutely necessary).

(d) Each purchase invoice might show the tax liability as well as the tax exclusive price in (b). This is not absolutely necessary as it is a simple operation to calculate the tax liability as a percentage of purchases. But where differential rates are in operation, it can be useful to have the tax liability shown on the invoices. This is common practice in European countries and in the US.

[7] Danish General Sales Tax: *Act No. 102*, 31 March 1967, article 15.

This information, when computerized, could be processed to give:

(a) Total domestic sales for each firm. As purchases by one firm are someone else's sales, the computer programme would select all purchases from the supplier bearing the code number X, and thereby collect total sales of the firm with the code number X.

(b) Customs would supply code numbers for exports (these could subsume (i) product classification, and (ii) destination codes). The computer programme would select those exports appropriate to the firm bearing code number X.

(c) (a) + (b) gives total sales.

(d) (b) multiplied by the tax rate gives the tax rebate on exports.

(e) Total purchases multiplied by the tax rate gives the tax credit on purchases.

(f) The tax rate multiplied by (a) gives the total tax liability on domestic sales.

(g) Subtracting (e) from (f) gives the net tax liability.

(h) Information from income tax returns will give wages and salaries paid by the firm.

(i) Annual total sales from (c) with annual total purchases subtracted will give value added which equals wages + profits.

(j) (h) subtracted from (i) gives profits, which provides a unique cross-check on company profits tax returns.

(k) Code numbers will give capital goods purchases (investment) (i) by goods, e.g., buildings, machinery, canteen facilities, roads, etc., or (ii) by industry, perhaps according to the Census of Industrial Production Classification, or some new and more detailed classification could be made. Exempt capital goods would be deducted from (e) above.

(l) Code numbers could produce sales of broad product groups monthly, quarterly, annually, (i) by region, (ii) by country of origin, (iii) by product grouping.

(m) Code numbers could produce imports, monthly, quarterly, annually, (i) by industry, (ii) by country of origin, (iii) by product grouping.

(n) Information could be processed to produce annual input/output tables.

(o) Information could be processed to produce regional input/output tables.

This is a Pandora's Box for statisticians. It could provide a most up-to-date continuous, series of statistics. The most obvious use is by the government especially in relation to checking tax evasion (see below), but also in planning, development, regional policy, etc. But it is also of great use to business.

At present, businessmen can only know how their firm is performing in relation to their industry, and relative to other firms and the national growth, about eighteen months to two years after the event. The Census of Industrial Production is annual and is published months after the collection of the figures. It is out of date before it is published. The information it provides, and the cross references, are sketchy by comparison to what could be possible under the flow of information from the VAT returns. Capital goods purchases would give information on a sector inadequately covered at present. But probably the most interesting and valuable statistical tool fashioned by the information from the VAT returns is the up-to-date, highly dis-aggregated input/output table. As the business uses of this are not widely appreciated in Britain (but are used increasingly in the US), some detailed explanation may be useful to emphasize the value to business as well as to government.

Input/output is a technique for measuring and analysing sales and purchases between the different industries in the economy. It is based on the simple principle that each flow represents a sale by one industry and a purchase by another (exemplified by the VAT returns), and that a change in one flow necessarily creates direct and indirect changes in other flows. This fundamental interdependence of industries throughout the economy is obvious, but difficult to measure by means other than input/output. This is the information which is almost uniquely provided by the VAT returns and is certainly provided in no other way which is so up to date.

The basic data required for input/output analysis are recorded on a large grid or matrix, which consists of a large number of rows and columns. Each row records the sales of each industry to all other industries, to final consumers, to government departments, and for exports. Each column records the purchases of each industry from other industries and from abroad. The sales of any one industry to any other industry may then be easily read off the grid. In this simple form the input/output table merely records all 'direct' transactions between industries.

However, the table may be used to derive various types of econometric models, which can be used to compute the indirect relationships between different industries. For example, a switch from coal to electricity as a source of power has obvious repercussions upon the demand for coal and electricity, but also affects the demand for timber, wagons, electric transformers, and insulating materials, etc. In turn, these changes affect other industries such as textiles, forestry, and iron and steel.

In summary, input/output forecasts provide a comprehensive profile of the structure of the economy at a future date, and form a valuable statistical and technological framework for management decision making.

The following types of problems are suitable for analysis by the general input/output forecasting techniques:

(a) The effects of changes in the level and compositions of consumer demand upon output and inter-industry sales and purchases.

(b) Analysis of the direct and indirect dependence of one industry on other industries.

(c) The likely consequences of technological changes upon inter-industry sales and purchases.

(d) Potential areas for product diversification and development in the light of changing demand and technology.

(e) The effects of government expenditure programmes, or the curtailment of such programmes, upon output and employment throughout the economy.

(f) General forecasts of output, employment, imports, and inter-industry sales.

(g) Effects of changes in fiscal policy and/or unit usage costs upon relative prices, demand, and output.

Another use is in inter-industry market analysis. Unlike general input/output forecasting which is based on an anlysis of the changing pattern of inter-industry sales and purchases through time, inter-industry market analysis quantifies the pattern of sales and purchases at one point of time. Input/output data are used to build up a market profile, analysing the different commodities produced by each industry and their sales distribution.

An analysis of this kind is extremely useful to the individual firms within an industry. By comparing the firms own sales records with the performance of the industry as a whole, areas of weakness and opportunities for increasing the market share of the firm can be identified, and marketing strategy formulated accordingly.

There are other applications of input/output which are not directly oriented towards business, but which are, nevertheless, important in relation to the economy as a whole. These include regional analysis, analysis of the effects of local authority expenditures, the collection and processing of official economic statistics, and special studies designed to evaluate government fiscal and expenditure policies.

Overall, the advantages of up-to-date statistical data are increasingly accepted by business, and the usefulness of such data is likely to grow. The VAT probably opens the valve to the most copious supply of accurate data Britain could have.

Nevertheless, it remains true that the body which gains most from the improved supply and quality of statistics is the government. Input/output tables, for instance, could be produced quickly and much more accurately than at present. Instead of being three or four years out of date, they might be produced within a few months of the end of the year. Moreover, they will be much more accurate. Tax bases could be calculated easily. Profits, sales, customs, and excise could all be accurately assessed.

Having said all this, it must be emphasized that to implement this statistical revolution would require a business revolution in itself. The vital information needed to produce the statistical cross-checks is the total purchases of goods and services on standard vouchers giving the suppliers code number (see above). The idea of multi-product firms supplying such information is, at the moment, far fetched. But if standard vouchers (automatically punched when the sale is made?) are used and wide product groups adopted, then processing can be completely computerized. It is by no means beyond the bounds of possibility.

However, it must be accepted that if a VAT is introduced into Britain in the next few years, such cross-checking would be unlikely, except, possibly, in the case of substantial sales to very few firms. If this is so (and the evidence indicates that it is), then a considerable amount of the statistical attraction of the VAT evaporates. The flow of information provided would not be appreciably better than that obtained from present taxation. Most important, the check on evasion would be greatly weakened.

Evasion

The check on evasion is an integral part of the tax. It is in the interest of every taxpayer to complete a return of his purchases so that credit for the tax content of these can be claimed against his VAT liability. If he omits any purchase, he cannot claim a tax credit on that purchase, therefore his tax liability increases.

A taxpayer might be tempted to under-report sales thereby reducing his value added and, therefore, his tax liability, but if the full statistical information described above were available, he knows that it is possible for the government to add up the purchases of his buyers and thus know his sales. This would be a severe constraint on any under-reporting of sales. Nevertheless, the under-reporting of sales, especially if the full statistics are not processed, or are dealt with inefficiently, does create a substantial gap in the EEC image of an impregnable VAT wall.

A *retailer* could certainly under-report sales since no automatic cross-check is possible. But the extent to which this is practical is limited. The authorities know the retailer's purchases, they can estimate his mark-up and, therefore, his potential sales. If he has not achieved these sales, then his stocks must have increased. If his stocks have not increased, then he is likely to be under-reporting.

In the previous section it was shown how under-reporting of profits tax liability could also be checked by abstracting total sales (from other companies purchases) and deducting purchases and wages.

But all this pre-supposes the full statistical model. If the sales of firms are not recorded with code numbers, and the only check on evasion is the desire to report fully all purchases, the restraints and examination of evasion are greatly weakened. There is no longer any way to assess one firm's sales by looking at another's purchases. Nevertheless, firms (especially public companies) may find it difficult to under-report sales, while the VAT certainly provides powerful encouragement to report all purchases.

If two taxpayers, by collusion, agreed not to invoice a transaction between them, the first party would have paid tax on his purchases which presumably he could claim against his other correctly invoiced sales, therefore he would not lose that advantage. The purchaser would acquire a product which had not been liable to VAT at the previous stage. But when he made his sale, unless it was again by collusion, he would have to report it for VAT liability and thereby bear the total burden of his own liability and the previous manufacturer's liability. This is the 'catching up' which makes evasion difficult. This self-enforcement fails if the final sale is a retail one. The non-invoiced sale between the wholesaler and the retailer could benefit both as the retailer, by under-reporting his sale, would reduce his tax liability. In turn, if the wholesaler came to an agreement with *his* supplier (a manufacturer), the tax burden could be reduced further. But clearly there are at least two checks on this process. First, it cannot be carried out for too many sales as the quantity of purchases for which tax credit will be claimed will look too large for the quantity sold. Second, the chain of responsibility is strung out and evasion becomes increasingly dangerous.

As far as the government is concerned, the evasion only puts at risk a fraction of the total yield of tax on that particular product. If a wholesaler and retailer successfully evaded the VAT, the tax liability on the value added up to the wholesale stage would still be collected. In this way, the potential cost of evasion is reduced compared to any single-stage sales tax, e.g., British purchase tax.

Where there are multiple rates of VAT, a trader might be able to take advantage of lower rates of tax liability on sales and claim a higher tax credit on purchases by a deliberate mis-classification of goods. This is another argument for as few rates of VAT as possible.

Finally, some evasion might occur if out-of-state companies carried out unreported services within the state, e.g., installation of machinery, consultancy, etc. This could put domestic competitors at a disadvantages. But such evasion should be small and the natural pique at such unfair practices could well bring the illegal activity to the attention of the authorities.

In general, it must be clear from the proceeding discussion that evasion under a general, fully cross-checked, VAT levied with few rates, would be difficult, would be open to considerable government checks, and would require the continued connivance of a large number of persons. The fewer the effective cross-checks, and the more rates of tax used, the less efficient the built-in anti-evasion devices of the VAT compared to more conventional sales taxes.

Fiscal policy

There are at least four ways in which the VAT can add to the fiscal weapons of government. First, as a broad based, general sales tax it is easy to use to raise large sums. This can give the government substantially greater freedom of action than it has in relying on relatively narrow based sales taxes, or on income taxes already levied at very high marginal rates.

The NEDO report questions the contribution of the present purchase tax as an economic regulator because 'there is no clear evidence that to increase it necessarily decreases *total* consumption in real terms while it discriminates heavily against particular industries'.[8] The VAT of course, since it is a more general tax, would tax all goods and services and not give people the chance to switch and buy tax free goods as they can with purchase tax. Their only tax free option would be to save in expectation of reduced VAT rates and lower prices. In that way, it could be a more efficient regulator of total demand.

Whether this is desirable or not depends on what a demand management regulator should do. The other side of the coin is to argue that cost push inflation is typified by bottlenecks in particular industries. This pushes up prices for those goods and hence the cost of living, and a wage demand inflation spiral starts. Specific taxation of those final goods where the bottlenecks occur or which are heavy users of materials which are in supply bottlenecks, e.g., consumer durables and sheet metal, can cut that demand without reducing demand in other sectors which still have a surplus capacity. In this way, growth of national output can be brought nearer to a maximum. If instead total demand is cut, then growth is sacrificed to stability; by cutting that demand selectively stability can be assured without sacrificing growth.

So runs the argument; on the one hand, the purchase tax is favoured because it is selective, on the other hand the VAT is favoured because it is not selective. If it is a multi-rate VAT, varying the rates and their relative position adds to the flexibility of demand management. Although whether this would be greater than at present depends on the structure of the VAT.

A combination of a broad based general VAT with multi-rates might combine the selectivity of the purchase tax with the advantages of the VAT. Of course, it creates many of the administrative difficulties discussed above, What is certain is that the impact of the VAT rate of change would be more immediate than a change in purchase tax. Producers at earlier stages of production would have to make decisions about whether to pass on the change in VAT liability. Under the purchase tax, it is only the wholesaler who has this decision to make. Increased revenue from a VAT rate increase would be obtained at once and business liquidity would be squeezed right down the chain of production, thus the full effect of a VAT change would be felt at once.

[8] NEDO: *Added Value Tax* op. cit., para. 3.19.

Moreover, since the VAT would be levied on a broader base, any change pound for pound would be more highly geared and have a much greater effect than a change in purchase tax.

Finally, the exporter could at once claim the full benefit of, say, an increased tax rate on his exports and thereby be at an advantage when buying intermediate materials, e.g., sheet metal, when competing with producers making domestic sales using the same intermediate material but whose sales would bear the full brunt of the tax on the domestic market. Of course, the same should be true for the exporter under a purchase tax.

Ironically, these advantages as an economic regulator, if they are considered advantages, could be reduced if Britain actually joined the EEC and was obliged to harmonize her VAT with that of the other members. A VAT harmonized in application, administration, and rates, would no longer be available as a fiscal weapon to a country in isolation. Even if the harmonized VAT were theoretically available as a joint fiscal weapon for the customs union, its use in practice would be difficult. It seems unlikely that countries with very different political and economic attitudes to budgetary stabilization policy would readily agree on simultaneous action;[9] such joint action on VAT as a flexible fiscal tool carries implications for joint action on expenditure and monetary policy.

There is a destabilizing effect of the VAT. The net VAT liability and the credit on purchases are both dependent on the amount of new investment. Investment is one of the more volatile influences in the economy. If there is an investment downturn, tax credits for investment will fall, and the VAT liability will rise. This means that the yield of the VAT will be rising as investment falls. The fall in investment is likely to be closely allied to a fall in demand and a rise in unemployment. These are not the conditions when the tax take should be increasing,

Another question is whether the VAT will act as a more efficient built-in stabilizer than the taxes it replaces. If it replaces existing single-stage sales taxes, as discussed above, it would be more general, and the full effect of changes in VAT rates—or alternatively business activity increasing value added—would be felt throughout the chain of production at once.

If the VAT replaces corporate income tax, its relative effectiveness as a built-in stabilizer is more complex. 'The value added tax would be a weaker automatic stabilizer than the corporate income tax, since profits are more sensitive to cyclical changes than value added. The loss in value added would be substantial.'[10] But further examination casts doubt on this statement. Whether the VAT has more automatic stabilizing power than the corporate

---

[9] Forte, F: 'On the Feasibility of a Truly General Value Added Tax: Some Reflections on the French Experience. *National Tax Journal*, December 1966, p. 67.

[10] Eckstein, O: 'European and U.S. Tax Structure', *The Role of Direct and Indirect Tax*, National Bureau of Economic Research and Brookings Institute, Princeton University Press, 1964, p. 247.

profits tax depends, like our previous discussion in chapter 7, on which shifting assumption is adopted.[11]

(a) If the VAT is shifted to the factors of production and investment is assumed as entirely exogenous or a function of output, the relative efficiency of the two taxes as automatic stabilizers is indeterminant.
(b) If the VAT is shifted and investment is determined by short-run profits as well as output, then the VAT would provide less stability than the profits tax, but
(c) If the VAT is shifted and the economy is at full employment then the VAT 'may give greater stability than the corporate profits tax'.[12]
(d) If the VAT is absorbed by profits, it will provide less stability than the corporate profits tax.

In general, therefore, the VAT substituted for a single-stage sales tax will improve built-in flexibility. Substituted for a corporate profits tax, it depends on the assumptions about shifting and the state of employment. As substitution is more likely to be for other sales taxes, the chances are that automatic stabilization would be improved.

The second fiscal policy implication of the VAT is more subtle. The credit on VAT paid on purchases of materials represents a cash claim on the government. Normally this can be offset against the current month's tax liability. There are two other courses:

(a) The period in which *all* tax credits can be claimed could be altered· If it is lengthened this represents an enforced (interest free) loan to the government by industry, and should be deflationary. If reduced, this represents an increase in the money supply and is expansionary.
(b) The period in which the tax credit on capital goods could be claimed might be altered (or that in which current goods could be claimed could be altered and the capital goods left constant). If lengthened, this could discourage investment. If shortened, it could encourage investment.

Both of these potential stabilization weapons would probably be difficult to administer. Both depend, in part, on the credit reaction of industry. Whether or not a firm claims the credit offset against its VAT liability on sales, the government does not require that the payment for the purchase on which the credit is claimed actually be made. That is, a firm can be claiming payments from the government which it has not seen itself. This is possible because the *invoice* is the determining factor in regulating VAT liability and

[11] Oakland, W. H: 'Automatic Stabilisation and the Value Added Tax', *National Tax Journal*, p. 41–60.
[12] Ibid., p. 57.

the claim for credit.[13] In this way, if a firm has been in the habit of immediate payment, when the government lengthened the period under which the tax credit could be claimed, the firm might then squeeze its suppliers for credit. However, as the VAT affects every link in the chain of production, every supplier would find his liquidity squeezed. So the change in the length of the VAT credit could be a most potent weapon for squeezing industry as a whole.

Another area where credit control could operate through the VAT would be in hire purchase. The government could demand the payment of the total tax liability as soon as the good was sold, even though the actual payment was to be made over an extended period. Or, at the other extreme, the government could charge the VAT on, for example, the monthly payments. This would then include a VAT on the interest payments unless the capital repayment and interest charge were clearly separated—which would be a welcome but at present unusual procedure in hire purchase. If the government insisted on total payment of the tax at the time of 'sale', this could be a squeeze on company liquidity. If it allowed the tax payment to be spread over the full length of the hire purchase agreement, this would be a relaxation. For flexibility, there are all the possible intermediate requirements.

A final credit adjustment which could operate as a fiscal control is the carry forward period when tax credits exceed tax liabilities. Countries differ in their treatment of this:

(a) France operates the 'buffer rule' which allows unlimited carry forward of excess credits, but which can only be offset against actual tax liability. There will be a net refund only in the case of exports.
(b) Germany allows any excess credit over DM 1000 to be claimed. Anything below DM 1000 is carried forward to the next month.
(c) The Netherlands operates like Germany, with a limit of DFL 1000.
(d) Italy proposes to roll-over excess credits to successive months like France, but will allow a net refund if there is an excess of credit remaining at the end of the calendar year.

These different usages could allow for differing effects on credit. If a government originally operated the German system and allowed more or less unlimited net excess refunds in any month, and then changed the law to allow a maximum of, say, 50% of total excess in any month to be repaid, the remainder to be carried forward to the next month, there would be a squeeze on company liquidity. By varying the percentage allowed, the squeeze could be relaxed or intensified. Other similar variations are possible.

The third way in which the VAT can add to the fiscal weapons of government is the speed with which the VAT is repaid to exporters and imposed on importers. If the VAT on imports is not payable until the end of the month, this represents a more liberal policy than if the importer could not collect

[13] International Bureau of Fiscal Documentation: *European Taxation*, Vol. 7., July/August 1967, p. 195.

his goods from customs until he could show his payment of VAT. In this way, there could be a credit control on imports. More unlikely, there could be encouragement of exports if the refund was reduced from, say, a month, to become instant. Denmark has adopted a very rapid repayment to exporters.

The two extremes for control on imports are first, the tax payment on imports before customs release of the goods, and second, a zero rate at importation and payment of the VAT liability incurred when the importer sells the product. Each has an advantage. If the tax is collected at the point of entry, the revenue is immediate and the risk of evasion is reduced, e.g., a final consumer cannot import a good without the sale being registered. But this also penalizes the importer who has to be out of pocket by the amount of the tax payment for a longer time than his domestic counterpart. Denmark tried to meet this difficulty by levying a 9% rate for registered importers instead of the normal 12·5% (a similar differential is maintained now the rate is raised to 15%). The alternative is to levy no VAT at import. But this gives the importer an advantage and also increases the risk of evasion.

Two methods are available to influence imports. One is that such a percentage difference as that operated in Denmark could be opened or closed in order to help or penalize importers. The other is, that importers while paying the usual rates should be given some longer period of time in which to pay the VAT to the revenue authorities. By varying the time period, imports might be affected.

Fourth, the VAT can be used as a backdoor method of altering exchange rates. In November 1968, Germany carried out what was tantamount to a revaluation, by using the VAT to tax exports (by not giving full credit on exports) and subsidize imports (by not taxing imports at a rate as high as the equivalent domestic products). Although this penalizes speculators and avoids the political embarrassment of changing the exchange rate (and presumably could be used in reverse to devalue), it makes nonsense of the neutrality of the VAT. As its neutrality is one of the main arguments in favour of the tax, to remove this neutrality greatly weakens the case for the tax itself. It is just as easy to have a retail sales tax and make it apply to exports as well.

If Britain wanted to alter the exchange rate of her relative trade position against, say, Germany, whether she used retail and wholesale taxes or VAT makes little difference. Both taxes are less efficient than a straight change in the exchange rate. Taxes can be evaded, particularly with long land frontiers, whereas it is most difficult to avoid the change in the purchasing power of domestic currency relative to other currencies. It also reduces the administrative clumsiness of what can only be a temporary expedient.

Clearly, the VAT could extend the range of government influence on demand, but the long term implications of EEC tax rate harmonization increasingly imply that discretionary alteration of such taxes, or manipulation of the conditions under which they are operated, will not be left to national governments. These decisions are more likely to be taken by the Commission.

Regional policy

As a sales tax, the VAT is not suited to regional variations. The EEC directives make no provisions for regional variations. Business opinion is against relating it to regional policy 'there must be . . . no attempt to marry it up with the Development Area legislation'.[14] This arsies from the extremely practical reasoning that, differential sales tax rates by regions create:

(a) A possible avenue of avoidance by out-of-region purchases.
(b) Complications in administration.
(c) Problems of definition.

It might be thought possible to vary the VAT rate according to regions at stages of production before the retail level. But if the tax is passed forward (as the directives assume it to be), then any lower rates will be 'caught up' at the retail stage when the full normal rate becomes due.

A more subtle technique might be to treat capital purchases differently in different regions. For instance, if the form of VAT adopted only allowed capital purchase tax credits to be claimed over the period of depreciation, e.g., VAT credit on buying a factory might be spread over ten years, then in the Development Areas this could be accelerated or allowed to be written off at once against tax liability. As other forms of regional assistance could be operated more directly (including the regional employment premium) at the same time as the VAT, there seems little point in using a new and unfamiliar tax for purposes which can be achieved in other less confusing ways.

[14] Rybczynski, T. M., Ed: *The Value Added Tax*, op. cit., p. 51.

143

10. The EEC experience of the value added tax

This chapter could discuss the operation of the VAT country by country. But this might be repetitious as the same problem is often met in a number of countries. For countries thinking of introducing the VAT and wanting to learn from the experience of others, it is more profitable to outline this experience in terms of common problems rather than to recapitulate country by country. The problems chosen for this chapter are: the introduction of the VAT; rates of VAT and fiscal policy; prices; treatment of capital goods, exports, and imports; the attitude of business; agriculture; the attitude of trade unions; and the attitude of government.

Some examples have been mentioned already, but this chapter is an opportunity to draw them together as an informative policy guide.

Introduction of the VAT

The deadline for the adoption of the VAT for all members of the EEC was originally set for 1 January 1970. Germany, France, and the Netherlands met this deadline; Italy and Belgium did not.

There is no single reason for this tardiness on the part of Italy and Belgium. It was easiest of all for France to adopt the EEC form of VAT. It was essentially a modification of her own tax structure that was adopted by the Neumark Committee as the EEC common sales tax.

The main difficulty in France was the extension of the tax to the wholesale and retail levels. Businesses which previously enjoyed extremely simple systems of tax assessment found they were obliged to keep a more complicated series of accounts. At the same time, the introduction of the new VAT was used as a convenient vehicle for simplifying many of the exemptions which bedevilled the old system of VAT. About fifty exemptions were abolished leaving only ten under the new tax. Various anomalies and forms of double taxation, e.g., on buildings and furniture, were removed. These were all improvements and were welcomed by the taxpayer. The government provided a comprehensive series of meetings to explain the tax and to advise on accounting systems and the modification of systems for handling the new tax.

Germany was anxious to ditch its inefficient cascade sales tax and also had a sufficiently efficient administration to push through the tax change by the same date as France, 1 January 1968. The Netherlands accomplished its change a year later.

But Belgium was reluctant to conduct the changeover at a time when prices were rising rapidly. Belgium would have preferred to introduce the VAT, as did Germany, at a time of minor recession. This means that the squeeze on firms might modify the extent to which they would pass the tax on at once. If the introduction of the VAT is made when other influences are forcing prices and costs upwards, businesses will be unwilling (and unable) to absorb a further cost increase. Even if the VAT was introduced at rates substantially lower than present taxes on some products, there would have to be increases on other products and relative prices would change.

Belgium was prepared to introduce the tax by the agreed deadline of 1 January 1970, but was put off by the experience of the Netherlands the previous January. Despite great care in the introduction of the tax, only two rates of tax, a strong administration, and a tradition of honesty among taxpayers, rapid price increases followed the introduction of the tax in the Netherlands and by April a price freeze had to be imposed.

In Belgium, the VAT is more complicated with four rates and the tradition is for tax avoidance rather than tax probity. The result was a decision to postpone the Belgian introduction of the VAT for a year until 1 January 1971. Some persons were caught out by this decision as they had purchased consumer durables in the full expectation of the actual introduction of the VAT in January 1970. Sales of cars were 12% lower in the first nine months of 1970 than in the same period in 1969, when there had been 'massive speculative purchases' in anticipation of the original date for introducing the VAT. In the event, in January 1971 everyone still expected prices to go up. This meant that individual actions combined to ensure that prices actually did rise. People rushed to stock goods in anticipation of higher prices. The initials TVA were associated with the slogan *tout va augmenter*.

This was hardly helped by the government's original intention which stated that rates would be fixed at 20% and 15% to yield a revenue surplus to that raised by the previous taxes. The assumption was that avoidance in Belgium would continue despite the supposedly evasion-proof security of the VAT. To ensure an equal yield, the rates had to be set higher than they would otherwise have been. The business protests over these proposed maximum rates persuaded the government to cut them to 18% and 14%, but the general business attitude was still to mark up prices on the basis that you are unlikely to be wrong if mark-ups are wider, but you could be very wrong indeed if mark-ups fell. Wholesalers and shops closed between Christmas and the New Year to make inventories, and stocks were generally run down. Consumer credit was kept extremely tight to reduce the surge of speculative purchases in anticipation of the introduction of the VAT in January.

The opposition of the Italians to the tax is compounded of more problems than elsewhere. It is associated with:

(a) Rising prices, as in Belgium.
(b) Difficulties with the retail stage.
(c) Administration in general, particularly a tightening over general widespread evasion and avoidance associated with a general recasting of the tax structure.
(d) Business opposition because of present export advantages.
(e) Basic opposition on theoretical and practical grounds.

The Italians agreed in 1967 to introduce the VAT on 1 January 1970, but indicated that they would not (could not) extend it to the retail stage. The Italian Ministry of Finance was unwilling to tackle the huge problems associated with taxing thousands of small shops, ill-equipped to calculate their VAT liability, and indeed unwilling to co-operate with the authorities. When, in December 1969, the Commission agreed to Italy's request for permission to postpone the introduction of this measure until 1 January 1972, it asked Italy as a *quid pro quo* to extend her VAT in 1972 to the retail stage. But the Italians are adamant on this point. They announced that they would use the escape clause in the EEC tax harmonization legislation under which the VAT may be introduced at the retail stage later than in the rest of the economy. 'Italy's Minister of Finance explained that his government favoured the extension of the VAT to the retail trade in principle, but believed that it should be phased over a period of time, as the large numbers of retail outlets in the country would make the introduction of the tax very costly to administer.'[1]

The Italians have also been bedevilled by the general problems of administration. The Bill to introduce the VAT is part of a whole package of tax reform. Moreover, priority is not given to the introduction of VAT but to income tax reform (one income tax replacing the present multiple types of income taxation). The introduction of VAT is combined not only with the removal of the municipal sales tax but with a galaxy of excises on, for instance, linen and woollen filament, matches, lamps, electricity, etc. With changes in government, the tax reform Bill has been held up and has to be re-introduced by each new government. Generally, the 'Italian tax administration is reluctant to venture into this new tax area'.[2]

Italian exporters may not be enthusiastic supporters of the new tax either. Under the existing cascade tax, average rebates have to be given for the tax content of exports. The uncertainty about the size of these rebates was one

---

[1] International Monetary Fund: *International Financial News Survey*, Vol. XXII, No. 1.
[2] Forte, F: 'E.E.C. Sales Tax Harmonisation: an Alternative Scheme', *Banco Nazionale del Lavoro*, July 1967, p. 60.

of the main forces stimulating the initial change within the EEC to the common form of VAT. It has been widely felt by other countries that Italy's tax rebates to her exporters were excessive, thereby forming a subsidy to exports. Because they were favoured by the uncertainty of the cascade system, Italian exporters knew they would be penalized, by comparison, under the new VAT. One way to speed the introduction of the VAT is to reduce the value of the cascade system to Italian exporters by reducing the size of the rebates. So, at the same time as the Commission agreed to extend the date for the Italian introduction of the VAT to 1 January 1972, it also persuaded the Italian Government to reduce its present export rebates. In this way, the reimbursement rates for cars was reduced from $7 \cdot 8 \%$ to $6 \cdot 5 \%$, for engineering goods from $7 \cdot 5/6 \cdot 5 \%$ to $6 \cdot 4/5 \cdot 5 \%$, for chemicals from $5 \cdot 5/5 \%$ to $4 \cdot 95 \%/4 \cdot 5 \%$, and for textiles from $5 \%/4 \%$ to $4 \cdot 5 \%/4 \%$. As they see any advantage they had from the old tax whittled away, businessmen may come to support the VAT, for at least they will know precisely where they stand under that tax.

Finally, the Italians have criticized the VAT on grounds very similar to those which appeared in the Richardson Report. They argue that although it is understandable that those countries with cascade taxes should want to change to the VAT, this should be seen as a steppingstone to a 'best' sales tax which is a single-stage tax.

Under the EEC scheme not only should single-stage tax countries be obliged to deteriorate their indirect tax system to join the Common Market; EEC countries' movements towards a better sales tax system should also be frozen. It is difficult to understand in what sense this kind of harmonization accords with the basic aim of fostering progress, which is set forth at the beginning of the Rome Treaty.[3]

The Norwegians suffered two defects from the introductions of the VAT on 1 January 1970. In the first place, consumers anticipated a general price increase when the VAT was introduced. They therefore tried to beat the tax by stepping up their purchases of consumer durables in the year before the tax was introduced. As there was unused slack in the economy, this did not produce any extraordinary rise in prices, but employment rose rapidly. If a government tried to introduce the VAT in a period when capacity was fully utilized, the speculation and comment of press and radio might well create a consumer boom which could spill over into prices even before the VAT was introduced.

The second Norwegian problem concerned the control of liquidity. The introduction of the VAT required a change in the date on which taxes were due and this created an unusual increase in liquidity in the private sector. The government had to take steps to neutralize this by increased government borrowing.

[3] Ibid., p. 65–66.

Overall, the Italians have had the most complicated reasons for delaying the introduction of the VAT. But generally all countries had at least one pre-occupation about the introduction of the VAT and that was the problem of price changes.

Prices

The substitution of the VAT for any other tax will not leave prices unchanged. Even if the yield of VAT is equal to that of the taxes it replaces, there are bound to be changes in relative prices. If the EEC 1969 Directive stipulating that by 1 January 1974 no member State would be allowed to use more than two rates of VAT is implemented, clearly there are substantial changes in relative prices to come as France and Belgium adjust their existing four-rate system to two rates. It is worth noting that Britain has agreed that the five-year transitional period for industry and agriculture will also apply to fiscal harmonization, including the introduction of the VAT. If this also means applying only two rates, very substantial changes in relative prices must occur.

The most successful containment of prices took place in Germany where, the changeover from a cascade tax at 4% to a VAT at 5% and 10% resulted in an insignificant price change. The changeover was intended to be an equal yield tax substitution, but some differential price increases might have been expected. However, the change took place at a time when the German rate of economic expansion had slowed down and so price increases were generally tempered. Small firms took the opportunity to raise prices by the full amount of the new 10% VAT making no allowance for the removal of the old cascade tax. But large firms saw little opportunity for increasing prices. 'Leading car manufacturers have kept their price lists unchanged, as have most book and newspaper publishers.'[4] Food prices dropped a little and the price of some services rose sharply only to be cut back by competition.

At the other extreme, Denmark and the Netherlands suffered price increases of 7·9% and 5% respectively attributable to the introduction of the VAT. In Denmark, the tax was expected to lead to a large rise in the cost of living. Food and services were to be taxed whereas previously they had borne little tax. Realizing the unavoidable substantial changes in prices, the government took the opportunity to re-organize the whole tax structure and made well publicized reductions in income taxes for lower incomes and increased allowances for those not liable to income tax. Large wage increases, just before the introduction of the VAT, helped to compensate workers for the price increases. But as discussed more fully below, the automatic index link between prices and wages caused particular problems for Danish fiscal policy.

In the Netherlands, the introduction of a VAT at 4% and 12% was forecast to increase prices by anything from 1·25% to 3·5%. In the event, both

[4] *The Economist*: 6 January 1968.

these forecasts were exceeded and there was an increase of 5% in the cost of living in the first three months after the introduction of the VAT. Less than half of this can be attributed directly to the new tax, however. What is believed to have happened is that traders took advantage of the general confusion to widen margins and mark up prices across the board. Within four months of the start of the new tax, the Dutch Government was obliged to introduce a price freeze and decreed maximum permissible price increases. Some businesses were obliged by the Government to reduce prices. The Netherlands provides a good example of a country which suffered from what might be called the 'Richardson's disease': that is, a rapid increase in prices promoting wage claims to maintain real incomes which, in turn, increase business costs and increase prices, further offsetting any gain there might have been for export prices. Wage demands following on the heels of the price increases pushed pay levels by August 1969 above the forecast for the complete year. The situation was such that the Government was obliged to postpone for at least six months its plans to increase the rate of VAT in 1970. This delay put considerable restraint on the budgetary freedom of the Dutch Government in 1970.

There are various effects on prices between the extreme cases of Germany and the Netherlands on the introduction of the VAT. In France, a VAT with four rates replaced the more limited coverage of a general 20% VAT. It was not an equal yield substitution but one which cost the government £130 million in 1968 in lower tax receipts. 'The cleaning and dyeing industries predicted increases of 5%; construction industries 10%; food products as follows: bread 5%, dairy products 2%, fruit and vegetables 3%; and varying increases for meat, clothing, automobiles, construction, champagne and mineral waters.'[5] Despite the lower tax yield, prices still rose by about 1%.

In general, the problems of price changes from the introduction of the VAT are of two broad types:

    (a) Those of changes in relative prices.
    (b) Those of a general price rise.

Changes in relative prices are almost unavoidable given that the VAT is substituted for quite different taxes and that the rates can only approximate to previous rates—especially if the *number* of rates is to be reduced. For instance, if the purchase tax is to be replaced by the VAT, to agree with the Commission directive the number of rates would have to be reduced from four to two. This, combined with changes in excises, would create numerous changes in relative prices even though the tax yield remains the same.

The factors affecting the general price rise are usually particular to the country. Much depends on the timing of the introduction of the tax. The Germans squeezed their businesses and stopped them increasing prices not so much by design but because the introduction of the VAT happened to

[5] *International Herald Tribune*: 28 December 1967.

coincide with a minor recession. Again, the Germans were fortunate that their VAT did not extend the tax base unusually; but in Denmark, because services and food were exposed to a higher tax rate, large price rises resulted.

The same phenomenon of price changes associated with the VAT is seen clearly not only with the changeover to the new tax, but with changes in the rates of the existing VAT. In Sweden, when VAT rates were increased in January 1971 (see Table 10.1), government action took two forms. First, to stop the rush of anticipatory buying of consumer durables, the higher new rates were accelerated and imposed nine months earlier than the general rate change. Second, to control mark-ups in the context of the price rise, the government imposed a six-month general freeze on the prices of all goods and services.

Of course, these measures characterize not so much the innate disadvantages of the VAT but rather the disadvantages of a parliamentary procedure which can give a year's notice of sales tax increases. It is simply asking for trouble to give consumers this sort of notice. Indeed, in a belated attempt to catch up on this, the Swedish Authorities had to advance the date of many of the tax increases on consumer durables.

The message of experience here seems to be that if price rises are expected because of an extension of the tax base and/or increased tax rates, it is best to combine the introduction of the VAT with an in-depth overhaul of the tax structure and plenty of publicity to convince people that their net position has not deteriorated. This might also be combined with careful government checks to ensure that traders do not use the uncertainty surrounding the introduction of the new tax as an excuse to widen margins. If possible, changes in tax *rates* should not be published beforehand; announcement and implementation should be simultaneous.

Rates of VAT and fiscal policy

The experience of Continental countries in altering their rates of VAT has all been in one direction—upwards. As Table 10.1 shows, the rates of VAT have risen in all countries since its introduction.

These increases are usually justified on grounds of management strategy in relation to internal domestic demand. But at the same time, it can hardly be doubted that the extreme bouyancy of the VAT makes it a very convenient revenue source as well as a demand management tool.

In France, the lowest rate is on staple foodstuffs, and the next rate on other foodstuffs, soft drinks, wine, coal, electricity, gas, housing, and services such as laundries, hairdressing, etc. The luxury rate applies to jewellery, yachts, cars, radios, and leisure goods.

Mixed up with the desire to use the VAT for demand management has been the opposite wish, to stop rate increases as they have an immediate impact on prices and hence are usually inflationary. Trade unions are now so well aware of the erosion of the real living standard of their members

Table 10.1

Changes in effective rates of VAT 1968/72 expressed as a percentage

		1968	1969	1970	1971	1972
Belgium:	Lowest				6	
	Intermediate				14	(15)
	Normal				18	(20)
	Luxury				25	
France:	Lowest	6·4	7·53			
	Intermediate	13·6	17·65			
	Normal	20·0	23·45			
	Luxury	25·0	33·33			
Germany:	Lowest	5·0	5·05			
	Normal	10·0	11·0			
Netherlands:	Lowest		4·0			
	Normal		12·0		14	
Italy:	Lowest	(10·0)*				(6)
	Normal	(15·0)		(10)		(12)
	Luxury	(20·0)				(18)
Denmark:	Normal	10·0	12·50	15·0		
Sweden:			11·11		(17.65)	
Ireland:	Lowest					(5·26)
	Normal					(16·37)
	Luxury					(30·26)

* Figures in brackets are proposed rates. Changes in rates do not necessarily correspond to calendar years, e.g., the German rates were changed in the middle of 1968.

through rising prices that wage claims backed by strike action are a quick response to increases in the cost of living.

This is especially true when the price increase is across the board and is seen to be directly related to a government decision to impose further taxes. Of course, the VAT has precisely these effects. Because of this we find reports in October 1969[6] that:

The fear of adding further to the upward pressures on prices has now induced the Government of the Netherlands to delay a planned increase in VAT from next January until July 1970, and has prompted the Belgium and Italian Governments to postpone their implementation of the VAT until January 1st 1971 and January 1st 1972 respectively.

[6] International Monetary Fund: *International Financial News Survey*, Vol. XXI, No. 43.

In this case, rate increases in the VAT were seen as necessary on some grounds, e.g., government revenue, but had to be postponed because of other undesirable side effects. The VAT rate changes have certainly not increased the flexibility of government fiscal policy.

On the other hand, VAT rate changes have been used as an alternative to other forms of fiscal attack and might thereby be thought to have increased the government's fiscal weapons. In the first quarter of 1970 the Danish Government, alarmed at the rapid expansion of domestic demand, strong price increases, and a record deficit on the trade account, proposed to suspend the automatic link between the index of prices and the index of wages and salaries. Some offsetting compensation for the loss of income would have been made in the tax free allowances. However, because the trade unions and the parliamentary opposition were against the suspension of the index link, the Government was obliged to turn to changing the VAT rate as a second best alternative.

The VAT rate was raised from 12·5% to 15% as from 1 July 1970. Unfortunately, this raised prices and, because of the index link, wages were increased to compensate. Perhaps in an endeavour to break this vicious circle, the Government proposed a temporary reduction in the employers' contribution to the general pensions scheme, to be made up by a government contribution. The *quid pro quo* for this might be an expectation that businesses should absorb part of the tax increase and thereby reduce the size of the automatic wage adjustment.

Clearly, the VAT in these circumstances is an unfortunate tax to use as it completes the circle of prices, wages, taxes, prices. . . . But this is not so much a criticism of VAT, but rather a comment on the undesirability of formally linking wages and salaries automatically to price changes.

The aim of the EEC to harmonize the rates of VAT would preclude the use of rate alterations for fiscal policy in any one country. The disparity of rates is still large with the 'normal' rate varying from Germany at 11% to France at 23·45%. Moreover, the rate differentials are even more significant. The difference between the highest and lowest rates in Germany is 5·5%, in the Netherlands 8%, and in France 25·8% (in Denmark, of course, it is zero). A harmonization of rates would produce substantial changes in relative prices. The desire of some countries to minimize controversial price changes may well inhibit progress towards harmonization of rates, as it has already done in the introduction of the tax.

The Swedes have used changes in the tax base which are equivalent to changes in tax rates. On the sale of buildings and prefabricated buildings, catering, hotel rooms, construction work, etc., the tax base is reduced to 60% of the cash value. With a tax rate of 17·65%, this reduces the actual rate to 10·6% on such transactions.

Similarly, on construction work involving water works, roads, streets, bridges, railways, harbours, canals, and services by architects, quantity surveyors, advertisers, etc., the tax base is reduced to 20% of the total cost and this reduces the standard rate of 17·65% to only 3·5%.

In this way, the Swedish authorities have been able in fact to levy three rates (3·5%, 10·6%, and 17·65%) while nominally having only one rate.

Experience has shown some difficulty in dealing with land. In Sweden if a joint price is put on the sale of a building and the land on which it stands and which goes with it, the taxable value of the lot is 60% of the total price reduced by an amount corresponding to the value of the land at the time of the sale. In this way, there is no VAT on any increase in the value of land.

Many countries might consider this a desirable treatment. But this distinction could provide a neat and useful way of taxing development profits from land speculation. There is an opinion in many countries that much of the appreciation in land value derives not so much from any entrepreneurship or risk by the owner of that land, but rather from a combination of social values. Various governments have tried to tax such increases in land values. The VAT could provide a neat way of doing this: if land was deemed to have been improved in value by public works in the nature of sewage and water provision, or the building of roads and communications networks, then the VAT could be levied either on the full sale value of the land if sold for development purposes, or on some percentage of that value. The same could be done where houses are sold with considerable land attached to them which is then used for development purposes.

Treatment of capital goods, exports, and imports

The EEC directive favoured the VAT as a pure consumption tax. This means that technically it should be a 'net value added tax of the consumption type' which requires an immediate refund of tax on all inputs including purchases of capital equipment.

This poses few problems for countries adopting the VAT if they already exempt capital goods from taxation. In practice, only Denmark has been able to switch straight to a pure net VAT. In general, four years have been allowed as the period when investment goods continue to be liable to a (diminishing) tax. If a country passes directly from a cascade tax to a VAT, investment goods would have been liable under the old tax but are not under the new; therefore, firms find it profitable to postpone investment and run down stocks in anticipation of the new tax. This could create very odd problems for capital goods industries and would be a distortion in the economy due only to a temporary freak of tax legislation. One way round the difficulty would be to compensate firms for the investment taken under the cascade system and on goods in stock, but in turn this would be difficult to finance except, possibly, by borrowing.

Germany, the Netherlands, and Belgium have transitional arrangements for capital goods (see chapter 7). Some odd marginal cases remain, the most vexed of which is the difficulty over cars used by businesses. A car bought and used wholly for business purposes is a capital good. Unfortunately, it is indistinguishable from a car that may be used only partly for business, or even not at all for business, even though ostensibly bought by and for the business. Continental practice in this is varied. Denmark allows a tax deduction on cars (and petrol) bought for business; where the car is used for both business and private motoring only 50% of the normal deduction is allowed. Germany and the Netherlands continue to tax cars under the temporary declining investment tax; presumably when this disappears, cars will be treated much as they are in Denmark. France and Sweden, on the other hand, do not allow any tax deduction for cars, but differ in their treatment of secondhand cars—France taxes them while Sweden does not.

Imports are supposed to bear the same tax as domestically produced goods at a similar stage of production. In practice, the interpretation of this has created considerable differences in treatment.

The main problem concerns the claim that when importers pay VAT on importing goods, they are paying out money at once, whereas the same goods produced domestically will only be taxed when they are *sold*. Hence there is some squeeze on importers compared to home manufacturers. There are two solutions to this. First the importer might be relieved of the obligation to pay tax until he sells his imported goods. This looks by far the most sensible course. The only problem is that it could lead to evasion (see chapter 9). The alternative is to levy a lower rate of tax on the imported goods. This looks a very poor option. It is impossible to know exactly what the rate of reduction should be—it differs for each article and even for the same article, depending on how long the importer holds the article and how long the domestic manufacturer holds the article. No two cases need be the same. Any rate correction would be arbitrary and might create more problems than it solved.

Nevertheless, rate reduction has been adopted as a solution by two countries. In Denmark, imports originally carried a rate of 7% compared to the normal 10% (which seems generous) and this differential has been maintained with subsequent increases in the normal rate. Sweden has imposed a 6·38% tax on imports of prefabricated houses compared to the normal rate of 11·11%. To be fair, neither of these cases is a simple case of relieving a liquidity squeeze on importers. In the Danish case, there is also an attempt to make some allowance for import levies. The question then becomes why have import levies if you then decide to have complicated offsets in your VAT? In Sweden, the reduced rate of 6·38% was about 60% of 11·11% which matched the *actual* VAT on buildings which were liable to VAT on 60% of their value. (The normal rate is now 17·65% and the reduced rate thereby becomes 10·6%.)

Another peculiar problem concerning exports and the VAT occurred in Belgium, where the Government estimated that as a result of the changeover to the VAT system, tax refunds to exporters would be some £75 million larger than under the old turnover rax. Rather than grant this expansion to exports all in one go, the Belgian Government decided to counteract this stimulus by a temporary export tax levied during the calendar year 1971. The revenue from the tax is estimated at about £37·5 million, so that exporters get half the advantage of the stimulus in 1971, and the other half in 1972 when the temporary tax is removed. In this way, some rough averaging is allowed for.

The final exceptional treatment of imports in practice has been the use by Germany of exceptional surtaxes on exports and reduced rates on imports as a means of hidden devaluation. From November 1968 to the revaluation of the Mark in 1969, goods imported and liable to the 'normal' rate of $11·11\%$ were allowed a refund of 4%, while those liable to $5·5\%$ received a refund of 2%. The same rates were applied to exports as a surtax. This, of course, was a peculiar use of the VAT and is not likely to become common practice.

The attitude of business

The attitude of business to the VAT can be dealt with in four main areas, the attitude of small businesses, the attitude of farmers, the experience of business revealed by appeals, and finally those points where business in general found difficulty in adopting the VAT system.

Every country has adopted its own rules to administer the VAT for small businesses. Table 10.2 gives a summary of these varying outlooks. It reveals the less frequent tax payment period for small businesses. Usually a quarterly payment has been found to be more reasonable for small traders. Norway made no distinction between small traders and others.

Sweden divided small traders into three sub-categories according to turnover, the smallest of all required to make only an annual return. Approximately 25% of all taxpayers are dealt with by putting them into the annual payment category; this means a substantial saving in administrative costs. Altogether, about half the total number of taxpayers are dealt with under the less frequent tax payment administration procedure. These businesses are kept fully within the ambit of the normal tax but are relieved from the responsibility of having to make frequent returns. On the state's part, all that is sacrificed is the interest on the revenue for two months. It seems to be a neat and simple way to reduce some of the administrative costs of the VAT.

Small traders are not obliged to adopt these special procedures; they can usually opt into the normal VAT system. In Germany, over 50% of small traders have in fact opted for the standard system. But something under 10% have done so in France. Naturally, once made, an option on the part of a small trader, to adopt the special system cannot be changed at will; some responsibility to run the system for a limited number of years must be accepted. In Germany and the Netherlands, a commitment for five years must be entered into, whereas in France the commitment is only for two years.

Table 10.2

Administration of the VAT for small businesses

	France	Germany	Netherlands	Denmark	Norway	Sweden
(a) Payment period for small traders (months) over usual payment period	$\dfrac{3}{1}$	$\dfrac{3}{1}$	$\dfrac{3}{1}$	$\dfrac{3}{3}$	$\dfrac{2}{2}$	$\dfrac{4, 6, 12}{2}$
(b) Administration of the VAT:						
(i) reduced taxation	yes	yes	yes			
(ii) *forfait* system	yes					
(iii) simple accounting procedures	yes					
(iv) application of normal VAT				yes	yes	

156

But in France, cumulative adjustments are made, on a rollover principle, on the basis of actual tax liabilities.

Apart from complete exemption, there are varying methods adopted to deal with small businesses that are not sufficiently small to be exempted completely, and yet whose size does not justify making them a part of the total VAT structure.

There are four methods used to deal with taxed small businesses (see table 10.2 (b) for a summary).

One way small businesses can be taxed is to ignore the complication of claiming credit for the tax paid on inputs. Instead, such businesses are taxed on their turnover at some rate lower than the usual VAT. With no tax credit to offset against their tax liability on turnover, this lower rate approximates to rough justice in taxing the small business. The trouble with this is that it mixes up a cascade element with the VAT, as exemplified in Germany where the lower rate allowed to traders whose annual turnover does not exceed £6800 is 4% of their gross turnover, which is the identical rate of the old multi-stage cascade tax.

The Netherlands has a similar system to Germany, but the French system is more complicated. A formula is used whereby the liability to VAT is subtracted from the limit under which the reduced rate can be claimed (£360 tax liability a year) and divided by three. This applies to approximately 400 000 traders. There is then a separate, and slightly more complicated, formula applied to very small craftsmen and artisans. This once more results in a lower tax rate which varies according to the actual turnover of the small business.

Quite apart from mixing up the concept of the VAT with cascade taxes, these reduced rates can also cause some injustice between firms, though the injustice would be likely to penalize the inefficient, i.e., those whose value added was lower than the average yet who were liable for the average tax on their turnover.

The Belgians adopted yet another way of using the reduced tax rate, although it is appropriate only for the small retailer. A small retailer is defined as a person who:

(a) Resells goods in their existing condition, i.e., he does not process them at all. This automatically excludes bakers, butchers, chemists, tailors, shoemakers, hairdressers, owners of small restaurants, etc.
(b) Does not sell particular luxury goods.
(c) Does not have purchases exceeding £12 400 a year.

When a retailer falls into this category, the responsibility for collecting the VAT rests on the supplier, the small retailer is thereby completely outside the scheme. The normal VAT applied by the supplier is increased by an 'equalization tax' fixed to correspond approximately to the tax which would be collected in the normal way from the retailer. The equalization tax is calculated in relation to the normal profit margin of the retail trade and its usual general expenses. Once more, this implies that the 'inefficient' small retailer whose expenses are higher than normal and whose margins are smaller, would bear more tax than his more efficient competitors, i.e., if he passed on this tax his prices would be higher than his competitors.

A second method is the *forfait* system which is unique to France and Luxembourg. This simply involves an agreement between the authorities and the small business as to what constitutes a likely reasonable tax liability over some fairly extended period. In France, this period is two years and the declaration is made by the trader during the second year. The declaration is based on the actual turnover of the first year. The assumption is that business conditions and turnover are unlikely to change abruptly over the period, therefore the first year can be used as a guide to the second year. On a roll-forward principle, if the actual turnover of the second year is remarkably different to the first, the state would have the right to make an adjustment upwards or downwards. All in all, the *forfait* system is simply a method of getting, for the authorities, revenue which otherwise might be lost.

Because of the complications arising from the multiple rates used in France, the authorities have introduced a simplified declaration of turnover for small traders and hotel and restaurant caterers. This system means that people in these categories no longer have to allocate purchases or sales to each of the individual tax rates.

In France also small businesses are given the option of tax assessment under the additive method instead of by indirect subtraction. That is, such businesses can opt to submit their accounts annually and be assessed on their value added of wages and profits. This was suggested as a desirable option by the Economic Development Committees of the printers and the food manufacturers in Britain.[7] Several difficulties occur. The annual assessment clearly gives an advantage to a producer assessed on this basis compared to one assessed on a monthly basis. The delay in tax collection allows the business a liquidity it otherwise might not have. Moreover, this option emphasizes the difficulty which is common to all definitions of small businesses, that is, they could be small one year but large the next, and then fall back into the small category the following year. Should the tax assessment be altered each year as the business grows or contracts? Normally, when a business opts to be treated under the special legislation for small businesses, it is then obliged to accept this treatment for a specified number of years. Of course, sometimes businesses find they are worse off under the special treatment than they would have been had they been fully part of the VAT system. Often businesses regret the choice they make.[8]

A particular business problem has been the VAT penalty on secondhand

[7] NEDO: *Value Added Tax*, op. cit., p. 86.
[8] Ibid., p. 34.

car sales (see earlier discussion in chapter 3). Most countries have found this a problem. They all want to make sure that cars are taxed at a high rate, but the higher the rate the bigger the incentive to sell secondhand cars privately, even to the point where cars are illegally sold 'privately' in Sunday sales in Continental market squares, so that by Monday morning the authorities are too far behind to catch up on any tax due. If governments are determined to continue to tax cars heavily the best solution seems to be a combination of a special excise on cars at the factory gate, combined with the lowest rate of VAT (with no credit allowed for the excise), thereby reducing the incentive to avoid the VAT by private sales between unregistered persons at the wholesale and retail levels.

A final way of assessing the attitude of business to VAT is to look for statistics on appeals against the tax system. Unfortunately, the tax has been in existence for too short a time in most countries for these figures to be available, and certainly not for them to be comparable one year with another. In Germany, such statistics are not obtainable for claims against particular taxes, but only as a total against all taxes. In France, cases heard by a tribunal which judges borderline disputes over VAT were 439 in 1968, and had dropped to 342 in 1969. Claims contested under the VAT structure had risen from 28 000 in 1968 to 33 000 in 1969, but of these those accepted had fallen slightly from just over half in 1968 to under half in 1969. In general the number of prosecutions for offences under the VAT system has been negligible, e.g., during 1969 there were 28 prosecutions, of whom seven were small businesses.

Agriculture

The special treatment of farmers is akin to that of small traders. The definition of farming is usually fairly wide including all normal tillage and livestock farming, but also fruit growing, horticulture, and forestry. Fresh water fishing is accepted in Denmark, Germany, and Norway but not in the Netherlands or France. There are special regulations where farming may be only part of a person's income. In France, if over 10% of the turnover is from non-farming activities then two accounts have to be run. In Germany, if more than 30% of a farmer's purchases are classified as non-farming activities, then he becomes liable to the full normal VAT, and is ineligible for the special treatment of farmers.

Table 10.3 gives a brief summary of the position of farmers in France, Germany, and Denmark. The number of farmers paying VAT appears to vary widely between, for instance, France with 134 000, and Germany with 23 000. This is largely illusionary. In Germany, farmers can opt to be treated, more or less, as consumers. This means that they are not liable to pay VAT and, therefore, are not included in the figure of 23 000. The German government has circumvented the problem of taxing farmers by neatly assuming that the VAT content on their purchases is equivalent to their tax liability.

Therefore, there is no net liability of farmers to tax. In France, farmers can be treated under a system where a global assessment is made of the likely tax content on their purchases as a percentage of their final sales, much as described in chapter 4. The usual rate of global credit offset is 2·4% and for livestock and poultry 3·5%. Much the same system operates in Denmark, so that both France and Denmark show a large number of farmers paying VAT.

The revenue from farmers, as shown in Table 10.3, is important to a country like Denmark but much less important to countries like France and Germany where the revenue as a percentage of the total VAT yield is under 1%, while for Denmark it is almost 9%. Farmers, much the same as small traders, can opt for a less frequent payment of tax. In France, they can pay tax once a quarter and in Denmark only twice a year.

Table 10.3
Farmers liable for VAT

	France	Germany	Denmark
(a) Farmers paying VAT	134 000	23 000	159 000
(b) Revenue from farmers (1969 £m)	17	12	31
(c) Revenue from farmers as a percentage of total VAT yield	0·3	0·3	8·6
(d) Payment period for farmers (months)	3	1	6
over usual payment period.	–	–	–
	1	1	3

A problem in all agricultural communities is direct sales by farmers to consumers. This problem of 'farm gate sales' is particularly acute in countries where the farming community forms a large percentage of the total population. In theory all countries, except Sweden, tax such sales. Clearly, it is extremely difficult to check these and claims that they are taxed must be suspect. The higher the VAT on agriculture, the greater the incentive for large numbers of city dwellers to flock to the countryside at weekends to buy direct from the farmer and cut out the tax on the wholesale and retail stages. The prospect of an army of agricultural revenue 'police' sniffing through the lanes of Sussex to catch the farm gate seller green handed is enough to encourage any administration to keep the tax on agricultural produce as low as possible.

Attitude of trade unions

It is precisely because management regards the tax favourably that trade unions might tend to look askance at it. Usually the substitution of sales taxes for corporate and business income taxes is bad news for the members of trade unions. Nevertheless, in most Continental countries the trade unions have seen it as a preferable alternative to the sales taxes that were in force. If such a substitution is to take place, unions must:

(a) Insist on full information on expected price changes and offsetting adjustments in transfers and income taxes.
(b) If price changes exceed forecasts, unions should press for further corrections in transfers and taxation.
(c) If many changes in relative prices occur, the temptation is to plead for numerous rates of VAT to avoid substantial price changes. It may however pay, in the longer run, to accept a more simple system with fewer rates, ensuring meanwhile that the offsetting income adjustments are made.

The cautious welcome of the Continental trade unions is not likely to be matched by British trade unions. The purchase tax to be replaced in Britain is efficiently and simply administered. The SET, which is criticized by many unions, could be replaced by a payroll tax. 'The Trades Union Congress, like the Co-operative Party, has expressed some fairly pointed opposition to the introduction of the value added tax.'[9] The suspicions remain that what management hopes to gain from the VAT cannot be what the trade unions want.

Attitude of government

Obviously the main task of government in introducing any new tax is to make sure that the public, trade unions, and management are fully informed of the various ramifications of the tax.

(a) The public and unions will want to have forecasts of relative and general price changes, and assurances (and examples) of the offsetting transfers to compensate, especially, lower income families for any increase in their cost of living. If prices are expected to rise, it is better to be explicit about it rather than to fudge the issues over a protracted period of wrangling.
(b) Businesses should be instructed in the operation of the new tax and, as in France, shown how to operate the changeover, while keeping margins constant. The emphasis on existing margins will bring home to them and to the public that no one is expected to 'make' out of these substitutions.
(c) Arrangements should be made to make the tax base as wide as possible. Every effort should be made to try to tax difficult areas, e.g., financial services and small businesses, by the annual accounts method (the direct additive method).
(d) Claims for exemption must be resisted.

[9] Morris, A: *Value Added Tax: a Tax on the Consumer*, Fabian Research Series, 284, March 1970, p. 20.

(e) The number of rates should be kept to a minimum (including different rates for imports).

(f) Governments must realize that acceptance of the EEC and its VAT implies a loss of budgetary revenue (because of the farm import levies and the 1% VAT transfer to the Commission central fund), potential loss of control over rates of tax and changes in rates, and, therefore, a dimunition of national parliamentary control.

Important points

From the European experience of the VAT commented on in various parts of this book, the following points should be mentioned since they are important to business. Businessmen should:

(a) Encourage the government to minimize the number of rates used. Most dissatisfaction has been expressed in countries using multiple rates. Administrative costs are higher and tax returns more complicated.

(b) Lobby the authorities to ensure that tax credits are granted at once and in full. Any carry forward of tax repayment is simply a loan to the government.

(c) Try to ensure that tax liabilities are kept up to date. Longer intervals between tax assessment also mean lying out of tax credits as these can only be claimed against tax liability. Ideally, of course, businesses would prefer instant tax credit claims and delayed tax liability, but this is impossible.

(d) Where capital goods have been liable to tax, ensure they are tax free under the VAT so that full and immediate credit is given for any VAT embodied in these goods. The 'buffer' rule as operated in France should be resisted.

(e) Watch the transitional arrangements carefully. The more complicated the tax substitution, the more difficult it is to calculate price changes. A substitution of the VAT for purchase tax would be relatively easy as all net of VAT prices of stages of production up to the wholesale stage would be unchanged providing four rates of VAT are used. The price between the wholesaler and retailer would be reduced by the purchase tax but would bear the VAT. This is all straightforward. If however, the SET or corporate taxes are also replaced by the VAT, then each buyer has to make an estimate of the extent to which his supplier ought to reduce his prices. After all, it is the power of the buyer that should stop businesses using the tax change as a lever for widening margins. Such calculations have to be made by each company individually. It was found in Germany that there was no point in actually going to suppliers for information which was often not forthcoming.[10]

[10] Rybczynski, T. M., Ed: *Value Added Tax*, op. cit , p. 37.

(f) Claim against the government for any stocks or capital goods on which tax has already been paid which are made free of tax. A close check should be kept on possible gains from careful inventory control in the transitional period.

(g) Ensure that all expenses are credited for tax contained, particularly where large staffs of travellers and representatives are maintained.

(h) If multiple rates are to be used, check carefully on the problem of negative 'catching up' (see p. 62–67) where credits are higher than liabilities.

(i) If large users of hydrocarbon oils, encourage the government to transfer part of the excise burden to the VAT to allow exporters to reclaim the tax content (see p. 106–108).

(j) If manufacturers, argue that they should be allowed to import, free of VAT, materials which will be used in production and then re-exported. This would follow the *regime suspensif* of France (see p. 91).

(k) Encourage the government to simplify the system of discounts. A common business practice is to give quantity discounts and these are often calculated on an annual basis. This means that sometimes there will be retrospective adjustments of prices between, say, wholesaler and retailer. There is, of course, little possibility of a change in the retail price of the goods, which are probably sold already and indeed were probably priced in the knowledge that there would be discount made. Therefore, if the retail value does not change, there is no change in the total VAT liability. There is, however, a change in the *relative* tax liabilities of the firm making the discount and its customer. If the VAT is passed forward fully this makes no difference to the firms concerned. At present, governments in the EEC require an adjustment of the VAT in respect of these annual discounts. It would be much simpler, and there seems no reason why it should not be done, if such retrospective price adjustments were ignored by the government.

(l) Be aware that a similar position holds when a container or other packing is returnable. Although the invoice showing the VAT liability may be technically misleading when allowance is made for the returned container, once more the change is only between parts of the total production chain and the total value added could remain unchanged. If the container is returned by someone who has bought the good retail, then there is an actual reduction in VAT liability. The amount is probably so small it can be ignored, or if industry thinks it important, reconciliation could be made on an annual basis.

(m) Ensure that full provision is made for reconciliation of VAT paid on bad debts.

(n) If it is thought company liquidity will be significantly stretched by the introduction of the VAT because of sales under extended credit, make out a detailed case to the authorities to obtain less frequent tax assessment.

(o) If conducting hire purchase business, argue, on grounds of comparability to the treatment of other financial services, that interest charges should be made free from VAT.

(p) Assess minor problems like ensuring that cash gift tokens are free from VAT (but VAT is collected on the invoice of the actual product purchased by the gift token) and make cases to the authorities, before the introduction of VAT.

(q) Emphasize the simplicity of tax forms requiring minimum information. What is needed is the tax rate on purchases for re-sale, on purchases not for re-sale, capital goods, etc., and on imports and the relevant tax rate on sales, self-deliveries, and exempt sales. It may be thought desirable to include, as a detachable part of the tax return, a pre-printed cheque to the authorities.

(r) Press for any exceptional transitional expenditure on machine accounting techniques, de-bugging computer programmes, etc., to be met by government from the exceptional revenue buoyancy it will enjoy on the once and for all extension of sales taxation to stages earlier than the wholesale. This claim could be made as a special credit against initial VAT liability.

(s) Help authorities to define 'small traders' and create flexible arrangements (annual or quarterly accounting methods, simplified tax returns) to deal with them.

(t) Set up an information service wherever dangers of evasion would affect companies, e.g., direct retail sale by farmers of their own produce.

In general, 'the management side of industry . . . regard the tax favourably, because it provides the Exchequer with an alternative to higher rates of direct tax on corporate and business income.'[11]

No one can maintain that the VAT is an ideal tax. There is no such animal. Like all taxes, it depends on what the alternatives are, on the time, and on the country. Perhaps the British single-stage sales taxes, even at high rates, on a broad general base, are more attractive. However, in the EEC this is not the option. Maybe a book should be written on the conversion of the VAT to a single-stage tax. But for the time being, it is hoped that this book will help to identify possible improvements in the VAT, and some of the important issues confronting those countries who adopt the VAT whether for love or necessity. Who knows? Like arranged marriages, necessity might burgeon into love.

[11] NEDO: *Value Added tax*, op. cit., para. 4.58.

Glossary

Accounts method: Also known as VAT by addition. Annual accounts are used as the main evidence for VAT liability. Wages and profits (after allowance for capital) are equivalent to value added, therefore, as profits are usually an annual residual, the accounts method of yearly assessment should reconcile with the monthly (usual) invoice method (see below and chapters 1 and 2).

Buffer rule: Net tax credits which represent a claim against the state, which the state does not repay but allows the taxpayer to carry forward to offset against future tax liability.

Captive goods: The possible advantage under the VAT to a registered manufacturer who absorbs an exempt stage and thereby claims credit on that stage's inputs whereas outside contractors cannot claim these credits (see chapter 3).

Cascade: When a tax is levied on a price which 'already includes a tax so that successive stages increase the tax liability and conceal the real tax element in price.

Catching up: If too little VAT is collected at one stage, it will automatically be caught at the next stage as the value added not previously taxed simply becomes part of the value added of the succeeding stage.

Country of destination principle: When products are taxed equally according to their place of final sale regardless of their place of origin.

Country of origin principle: When every good is taxed regardless of where it is bought so that each product reflects the taxes of the country of its origin.

Customs union: An agreement between countries to reduce customs duties while establishing a common external tariff.

Delivery: The technical term under the VAT structure which determines tax liability.

Dumping: Selling goods abroad at prices lower than those at which the same goods sell in the home market.

Elasticity of demand: The responsiveness of demand to changes in price, that is, the percentage change in the quantity demanded of a good or service divided by the percentage change in price.

FIFO: 'First In, First Out,' the equivalent for stocks of historical costing of assets (see below), where stocks are valued at the price of purchase rather than on the basis of the cost of the last item bought (Last In, First Out . . . LIFO).

Forfait: A bilateral agreement between the taxpayer and government as to the likely tax liability.

GATT: The General Agreement on Tariffs and Trade. An association of the major trading nations formed to try to reach agreements on reducing impediments to trade.

Global credit offset: An estimate of the VAT content of farm purchases expressed as a percentage of farm sales; used by the purchaser of farm output to determine the VAT liability of the farming stage (see chapter 4).

Historical basis of costing: When assets are valued at their purchase price, which during an inflation will understate their value compared to their replacement cost.

Input/output analysis: A means of measuring interrelations between sectors of the economy; input/output tables (or matrices) show the sales of one industry as the inputs of another.

Invoice method of VAT assessment: Also known as VAT by subtraction. Invoices are used as the main evidence of VAT liability, so that VAT is liable on all invoiced sales, against which the tax content of all invoiced purchases can be offset (see chapter 1).

Money illusion: When taxpayers do not attempt to maintain their real consumption of goods and services despite changing prices.

Occulte taxe: See *Taxe opaque*.

Opaque taxe: See *Taxe opaque*.

Progressive: When the percentage of tax deducted rises proportionately more than the increase in incomes.

Regime suspensif: When an exporter obtains raw materials free of VAT for the goods he intends to export. He thereby works with tax free materials.

Registration: Taxable persons under the VAT will have to be registered and have registration numbers.

Regressive: When the percentage tax taken rises proportionately less than the increase in incomes.

Retail: The sale of goods or services to the public in small quantities, usually through shops.

Sales tax: A tax, either expressed as a percentage of price or as a specific amount per article, on the sale of goods or services.

Services: Giving or selling advice or assistance where no physical transfer of ownership of goods takes place, e.g., banking, transport.

Shifting: The idea that the burden of tax can be moved from the person who ostensibly pays the tax either forward to the person who buys from the original taxpayer, or backwards to the person who sells to the original taxpayer.

Single-stage sales tax: A tax levied on the sale of goods or services at one stage in production only, e.g., wholesale or retail, and contrasted to a multi-stage tax which is levied on successive stages of production.

Taxe opaque: A sales tax which enters into the cost of production, particularly for exports, and which cannot be identified for refund.

Transfers: Payments by government to the private sector which increase disposable incomes, e.g., old age pensions, interest on the national debt, etc.

TVA: *Taxe sur la Valeur Ajoutée*. The name coined by Monsieur Lauré in 1954 to describe the French form of VAT.

VAT by addition: See accounts method (and chapters 1 and 2).

VAT by subtraction: See invoice method (and chapters 1 and 2).

Vertical integration: Integrating the steps in production from the suppliers to the purchasers of a manufacturer's output. Thus the control of raw materials and the sale of goods are covered.

Wholesale: The sale of goods in large quantities, usually for re-sale by the retailer to the public.

Bibliography

Aaron, H: 'The Differential Price Effects of a Value-Added Tax', *National Tax Journal*, June 1968.

Aliber, R. Z. and Stein H: 'U.S. Exports and Taxes', *American Economic Review*, September 1964.

Bracewell-Milnes, J. B: 'Value Added Taxation in the United Kingdom', *Journal of Business Finance*, June 1969.

Bradley, J. S: 'The Tax on Value Added', *Accountancy*, June 1969.

Break, G. and Rolph, E: *Public Finance*, New York 1961.

Bronfenbrenner, M. and Kogiku, K: 'The Aftermath of the Shoup Tax Reforms,' *National Tax Journal*, September/December 1957.

Bronfenbrenner, M: 'Second Thoughts on Value Added Taxation', *Finanzarchiv*, N.F., Band 16, Heft. 2.

Brown, C. V: *Impact of Tax Changes on Income Distribution*, PEP, February 1971.

Buyler, E. B: 'Britain and the Continental Value Added Tax, I and II,' *Bankers Magazine*, May/June 1968.

Central Statistics Office: *National Income and Expenditure, 1965*, Pr. 9379, Stationery Office, Dublin.

Chancellor of the Exchequer: *Value Added Tax*, HMSO, London, March 1971.

Commission on Income Taxation: *Third Report*, Pr. 5567, Stationery Office, Dublin.

Commission of the European Communities: *Proposal for a Directive on Application of the Tax on Value Added to Turnover in Agricultural Products*, Spokesman's Group: Press Release, Brussels, 23 February 1968.

Committee of Inquiry into the Impact of Rates on Households: *Report*, Cmnd. 2582, HMSO, London, February 1965.

Committee on Turnover Taxation: *Report*, Cmnd. 2300, HMSO, March 1964. (The Richardson Committee.)

Committee of the EEC Fiscal and Financial: *The E.E.C. Reports on Tax Harmonisation*, International Bureau of Fiscal Documentation, Amsterdam, 1963. (The Neumark Report.)

Council of the EEC: First Directive, 'For the Harmonisation among Member States of Turnover Tax Legislation', *Journal Officiel des Communautes Europeenes*, No. 71, Brussels, 14 April 1967.

Council of the EEC: Second Directive, 'On the Form and Methods of Application of the Common System of Taxation on Value-Added,' *Journal Officiel des Communautes Europeenes*, No. 71, Brussels, 14 April 1967.

Council of the EEC: Proposed Third Directive, *Terms and Conditions for the Common Application of the Tax on Value Added to Operations Related to Agricultural Products*, Brussels, February 1968.

Dale, A: *Tax harmonization in Europe*. Taxation Publishing Co., London, 1963.

Danish General Sales Tax: *Act No. 102*, 31 March 1967.

Denison, E. F: *The sources of economic growth in the United States*. Committee on Economic Development, New York, 1962.

Dionant, R. Van, Loeckx, F., and Neyens, G: *Elements de la Science des Imports*, Ministere des Finances, Belgium, 1962.

Dooley, O. S: 'Reactions of Selected United States Companies to the European Common Market', Temple University Economics and Business Bulletin, June 1965.

Dosser, D: 'Theoretical Considerations for Tax Harmonisation', *Comparisons and Harmonisation of Public Revenue Systems*, International Institue of Public Finance, Brussels, 1966.

Dosser, D: 'Economic Analysis of Tax Harmonisation' in Carl S. Shoup, ed, *Fiscal harmonisation in common markets*, Columbia University Press, New York, 1967.

Dosser, D: 'Welfare Effects of Tax Unions', *Review of Economic Studies*, June 1964.

Dosser, D. and Han, S. S: *Taxes in the E.E.C. and Britain: The Problem of Harmonisation*, PEP, London, 1968.

Due, J. F: 'Sales Taxation and the Consumer', *The American Economic Review*, December 1963.

Due, J. F: 'Should the Corporation Income Tax be Replaced by the Value Added Tax?', *Proceedings of the 57th National Tax Conference 1964*, National Tax Association, 1965.

Ebel, R. D. and Papke, J. A: 'A Closer Look at the Value Added Tax: Propositions and Implications', *Proceedings, 60th National Tax Association Conference*, 1967.

Ebel, R. D: 'The Michigan Business Activities (Value Added) Tax: A Retrospective Analysis and Evaluation', *Proceedings, 61st National Tax Association Conference*, 1968.

Eckstein, O: 'European and U.S. Tax Structure', *The Role of Direct and Indirect Tax Structures*, National Bureau of Economic Research and Brookings Institute, Princeton University Press, 1964.

Edwards, C. T: 'A Value Added Tax?' *Malayan Economic Review*, October 1968.

Fellner, W: 'Comment' on 'Taxation. Resource Allocation Welfare,' by A. C. Harberger in *The Role of Direct and Indirect Taxes in the Federal Revenue System*. Brookings Institution, Washington, DC, 1964.

Forte, F: 'On the Feasibility of a Truly General Value Added Tax: Some Reflections on the French Experience', *National Tax Journal*, December 1966.

Forte, F: 'E.E.C. Sales Tax Harmonisation: an Alternative Scheme', *Banco Nazionale de Lavoro*, July 1967.

Frapsauce, M: *Comment Appliquer la Nouvelle T.V.A.* J. Delmas et cie, Paris, 1968.

Friedlaender, A. F: 'Indirect Taxes and Relative Prices', *Quarterly Journal of Economics*, February 1967.

Graaf. J. DeV: 'The Future of Taxation', *South African Journal of Economics*, September 1968.

Geary, R. C. and Pratschake, J. L: *Some Aspects of Price Inflation in Ireland*, Economic and Social Research Institute, Paper No. 40, Dublin.

Goffin, R: 'An Account of T.V.A. in Belgium', *Bulletin of International Fiscal Documentation*, August 1970.

Gordon, R. J: 'The Incidence of the Corporation Income Tax in U.S. Manufacturing, 1925–62', *American Economic Review*, September 1967.

Hamberg, D: 'Fiscal Policy and Stagnation Since 1957', *Southern Economic Journal*, June 1963.

Harberger, A. C: 'Taxation, Resource Allocation, and Welfare' in *The Role of Direct and Indirect Taxes in the Federal System*, Princeton University Press, Princeton, 1964.

Harberger, A. C: 'A Federal Tax on Value-Added' in *The Taxpayer's Stake in Tax Reform*, Chamber of Commerce of the US, Washington, DC, 1968.

Harberger, A. C: 'TVA and Prices', *Bulletin of International Fiscal Documentation*, February 1968.

Ilersic, A. R: 'Value-Added Tax for the United Kingdom?' *Canadian Tax Journal*, November/December 1969.

Ito, H: 'Theorie und Technik der Nettoumsatzsteur in Japan,' *Finanzarchiv*, 1955.

International Bureau of Fiscal Documentation: *European Taxation: Netherlands*, November/December 1968.

International Bureau of Fiscal Documentation: *European Taxation: The Common System of Tax on Value Added*, Amsterdam, July/August, 1967.

International Monetary Fund, *International Financial News Survey*, Vol. XXI, No. 43.

International Monetary Fund, *International Financial News Survey*, Vol. XXII, No. 1.

Jansen, J: *Harmonisation of Turnover Taxes in the E.E.C.*, text of a lecture in Dublin, 14 September 1967.

Kaldor, N: *An Expenditure Tax*, Unwin, University Books, London, 1955.

Kaldor, N: 'A Memorandum on the Value Added Tax', *Essays on Economic Policy*, Volume 1, Duckworth, London, 1964.

Krzyzaniak, M. and Musgrave, R. A: *The Shifting of the Corporation Tax*, Johns Hopkins Press, Baltimore, 1962.

Laure, M: *La taxe sur la valeur ajoutée*, Recueil Sirey, Paris, 1952.

Leser, C. E. V: 'The Problem of Personal Expenditure in Ireland', *Bulletin of Statistical and Social Inquiry Society of Ireland*, Vol. 21, part 2, Dublin 1963/64.

Leser, C. E. V: *A Further Analysis of Irish Household Budget Data*, Economic and Social Research Institute, Paper No. 23, 1964.

Lindholm, R. W: 'A plea for the Value Added Tax', *Tax Review*, May 1969.

Lindholm, R. W: 'National Tax System and International Balance of Payments', *National Tax Journal*, June 1966.

Lindholm, R. W: 'Some Value-Added Tax Impacts on the International Competitiveness of Producers', *Journal of Finance*, September 1968.

Lindholm, R. W: 'Value Added Tax vs. Corporation Income Tax', *Business Economics*, January, 1970.

Lindholm, R. W: 'The Value Added Tax: a Short Review of the Literature', *The Journal of Economic Literature*, 1970, p. 1178–1189.

Lock, C. W: ' An Administrator's Point of View on the Value-Added Tax' in *Alternatives to Present Federal Taxes*. Tax Institute of America, Princeton 1964.

Loeb, C. W: 'Value-Added Taxation in States', *Proceedings of 61st Annual National Tax Association Conference*, 1968.

Loeckx, F., Van Dionant, R. and Neyens, G: *Elements de la Science des Imports*, Ministere des Finances, Belgium, 1962.

Mackintosh, A. S: *The Development of Firms*, Cambridge University Press, 1963.

Matthiasson, B: 'The Value-Added Tax', *Finance and Development*, March 1970.

McGuire, M. C. and Aaron, H: 'Efficiency and Equity in the Optimal Supply of a Public Good', *Review of Economics and Statistics*, February 1969.

McKinnon, R. I: 'The Value-Added Tax for Singapore: Rejoinder', *Malayan Economic Review*, April 1967.

Meade, J. E: *Problems of economic union*, Allen and Unwin, London, 1953.

Meade, J. E: *Efficiency, Equality and the Ownership of Property*, Allen and Unwin, London, 1965.

Merrett and Monk: *Bulletin of the Oxford Institute of Economics and Statistics*, August 1966.

Messers, K: 'Border Tax Adjustments', *The OECD Observer*, October 1967.

Minister for Finance: *Proposals for a Value Added Tax*, Revenue Commissioners, Dublin, March 1971.

Ministry of Finance: Denmark, *General Sales Tax (Tax on Value Added)*, Copenhagen, June 1970.

Missorten, W: 'Some Problems in Implementing a Tax on Value Added', *National Tax Journal*, December 1968.

Mitton, A: 'A Tax for our Time', Conservative Political Centre, London 1968.

Moller, M. E: 'On the Value-Added Tax in Denmark and the European Economic Community and the Renaissance of Tax Neutrality', *Bulletin of International Fiscal Documentation*, October 1967.

Moller, M. E: 'International Trade of Goods and Services with the TVA in Operation', *Bulletin of International Fiscal Documentation*, July, August, September, 1969.

Morris, A: *Value Added Tax: a Tax on the Consumer*, Fabian Research Series, 284, March 1970.

Musgrave, R. A: 'Tax Policy', *Review of Economics and Statistics*, May 1964.

Musgrave, R. A: *The Theory of Public Finance*, McGraw-Hill, London, 1958.

Musgrave, R. A. and Krzyaniak, M: *The Shifting of the Corporation Tax*, Johns Hopkins Press, Baltimore, 1962.

National Economic Development Office: *Value Added Tax*, HMSO, London, 1969.

Netherlands, 'Tax on Value Added', *Supplement to Bulletin for International Fiscal Documentation*, 5 August 1969.

N umark, F: *Neumark Report on the Fiscal and Financial Committee on Tax Harmonization in the Common Market*, Commerce Clearing House, Chicago, 1963.

Neyens, G., Loeckx, F. and Dionant, R. Van: *Elements de la Science des Imports*, Ministere des Finances, Belgium, 1962.

Niehus, R. J: 'The German Added Value Tax—Two Years After', *Taxes, The Tax Magazine*, September 1969.

Oakland, W. H: 'Automatic Stabilisation and Value-Added Tax' in *Studies in Economics Stabilization*, A. Ando et al, eds. The Brookings Institution, Washington, DC, 1968.

Oakland, W. H: 'The Theory of the Value-Added Tax', *National Tax Journal*, June 1967.

Oakland, W. H: 'Automatic Stabilisation and the Value Added Tax', *National Tax Journal.*

OECD, *Border Tax Adjustments and Tax Structures*, Paris, 1968.

Papke, J. A: 'Michigan's Value Added Tax After Seven Years', *National Tax Journal*, December 1960.

Pasinetti, L. L: 'Rate of Profit and Income Distribution in Relation to the Rate of Economic Growth', *Review of Economic Studies*, October 1962.

Peacock, A. T: *Income Re-Distribution and Social Policy*, Cape, London, 1954.

Peloubet, M. E: 'European Experience with Value Added Taxation', *Alternatives to Present Federal Taxes*. Tax Institute of America, Princeton, 1964.

Prest, A. R: 'The E.E.C. Value Added Tax and the U.K.', *District Bank Review*, London, 1967.

Prest, A. R: 'A Value Added Tax Coupled with a Reduction of Taxes on Business Profits', *British Tax Review*, 1963.

Reason, L: 'Estimates of the Distribution of Non-Agricultural Incomes and Incidence of Certain Taxes', *Journal of the Statistical and Social Inquiry Society of Ireland*, Vol. XX, 1960–61.

Reddaway, W. B: *Effects of the Selective Employment Tax, First Report, the Distributive Trades*, HMSO, London, 1970.

Revenue Commissioners: *Added Value Tax*, Stationery Office, Dublin, 1968.

Rolph, E. R. and Break, G: *Public Finance*, Ronald Press, New York, 1961.

Rolph, E. R: 'The Economic Effects of the Value Added Tax', *Excise Tax Compendium*, Committee on Ways and Means, Congress of US, Washington, DC, 1964.

Rybczynski, T. M., ed: *The Value Added Tax: the U.K. Position and the European Experience*, Basil Blackwell, Oxford, 1969.

Sandberg, S. G: 'A Value-Added Tax for Sweden', *National Tax Journal*, 1965.

Schirm, M: 'The Value-Added Tax in Germany' in *Value Added Tax: the UK Position and the European experience*, T. M. Rybczynski, ed., Blackwell, Oxford, 1969.

Schmidt, H. K: *Added Value Tax Law: English-German Text with Short Introduction.* Dr O. Schmidt, Köln, 1967.

Schmolder, G: *Turnover Taxes*, International Bureau of Fiscal Documentation, Amsterdam, 1966.

Shone, Sir Robert: 'Planning and Fiscal Strategy', *National Provincial Bank Review* London, 1968.

Shone, Sir Robert: Foreword to *Value Added Tax: the UK position and the European experience*, T. M. Rybczynski, ed., Blackwell, Oxford, 1969.

Shoup, C. S: 'Consumption Tax, and Wages Type and Consumption Type of Value-Added Tax', *National Tax Journal*, June 1968.

Shoup, C. S: 'Theory and Background of the Value-Added Tax', *Proceedings of 48th National Tax Association Conference*, 1955.

Shoup, C. S: *Fiscal Harmonisation in Common Markets*, Columbia, New York, 1967.

Shoup, C. S: 'Value Added Tax Experience in Denmark and Prospects in Sweden', *Finanzarchiv*, Vol. 28, No. 2, 1969.

Simpson, F. S: 'The Concept of "Fiscal Drag" and its Relevance to the Tax "Bulge" in South Africa', *South African Journal of Economics*, June 1968.

Slitor, R. E: 'The Role of Value-Added Taxation in the Tax Structure of the States: Prospective Developments', *Proceedings, 61st National Tax Association Conference*, 1968.

Smith, D. T: *Effects of Taxation: Corporate Financial Policy*, Harvard University Graduate School of Business Administration, Boston, 1952.

Stout, D. K. and Turvey, R: 'Value Added Taxation, Exporting and Growth', *British Tax Review*, September/October 1962.

Stout, D. K: 'Economic Aspects of the Value Added Tax in the U.K.' in *Value Added Tax: the UK position and European experience*, T. M. Rybczynski, ed., Blackwell, Oxford, 1969.

Sullivan, C. K: 'Concepts of Sales Taxation' in *Readings on Taxation*, Richard Bird and Oliver Oldman, eds., The Johns Hopkins Press, Baltimore, 1964.

Sullivan, C. K: *The search for tax principles in the European Economic Community*. International Program in Taxation, Harvard Law School, Cambridge, Mass., 1963.

Sullivan, C. K: *The Tax on Value Added*, Columbia University Press, New York, 1965.

Swedish Ministry of Finance: *The Swedish Value Added Tax*, Government Publication, April 1969.

Tait, A. A: 'Deflation and Incomes Policy: The British Budget 1968/69', *Finanzarchiv*, October 1968.

Tait, A. A: *The Economic Consequences of Introducing a Value Added Tax into Ireland on the E.E.C. model, covering Industrial Production, Agricultural Production, and Services*. Paper for the Economic and Social Research Institute, April 1969.

Ta-Yeh, W: 'McKinnon's Value-Added Tax and Industrial Development in Singapore', *Malayan Economic Review*, October 1968.

Wheatcroft, G. S. A: 'Some Administrative Problems of an Added Value Tax', *British Tax Review*, September/October 1963.

Index

176

Excise rates:
  harmonised, 111
Excises:
  adjustment under VAT, 79
  in Britain compared to Continent, 58–61
  at different rates in Europe, 111
  not rebated on exports, 111
  replaced by VAT, 111–114
  and transition to VAT, 131
Exempt:
  persons who are partly, 32
Exemptions:
  claims for resisted, 161
  total, 20–23
  and transitional Board, 131
Expenses credited for tax, 163
Exports:
  agricultural, 52, 53
  incentive to, 34
  prices and SET, 115
  problem of agricultural, 52
  and psychological attitude, 91
  subsidy of, 18
  surtaxes on, 155
  tax rebates, 8, 154, 155
  tax rebates in Italy, 146, 147
  taxes on, 17
  and value added, 19
  and VAT base, 33, 34
  and the zero rate, 32
Exporters:
  repayment of VAT, 141

Factor substitution:
  and VAT absorbed, 67
Factories:
  old and efficiency, 103
Farm machinery, 53
Farmers:
  combined with other business, 159
  and exemption, 20, 42
  payment period, 160
  revenue from, 160
  as small traders, 159
Fertilizers, 51
FIFO, 99
Financial deduction, The, 6
Financial transactions:
  taxed by additive method, 21, 22
Firms:
  price lists and taxes, 87
Fiscal policy:
  effects of changes in, 135
  and VAT, 138–143
Fishing, 51
Fixtures:
  installation liable to VAT, 27

Food:
  British policy of cheap, 79
  exemption of, 51
  higher taxes on, 113
  and low rates, 57
  tax liability, 82
Footwear:
  price changes, 86
Forestry, 51
Forfait:
  small retailers, 35
  system, 156
Forms:
  simplicity for tax returns, 164
Forwarding, 23, 25
Fractional payments, 8
Fractionated tax, 19
France:
  and additive method, 158
  adjustments in tax base instead of tax rates, 62
  adoption of VAT, 144
  appeals against VAT, 159
  "buffer" rule, 99, 141, 162, 165
  and carry forward period, 141
  cars for business, 154
  changes in relative prices through harmonisation, 68
  changes in VAT, 151
  complaints of protectionism, 15
  and corporate income tax, 104
  definition of farmer, 159
  definition of small business, 38
  entertainment and VAT, 29
  and Forfait system, 158
  lowest rate, 150
  and luxury rate, 56, 150
  and multiple rates, 65, 66
  number of farmers, 159
  number of taxpayers, 124
  proportion of revenue from VAT, 69
  and retail stage, 36
  retailers, 35
  sales tax content of alcohol and tobacco, 112
  and small traders, 155
  social security contributions, 120
  tax documents, 126
  tax inclusive of VAT, 3, 12
  tax on financial services, 22
  tax period, 128
  transitional problems for investment, 88
  VAT designed to encourage shifting, 97
  visits to traders, 127
  youth hostels, 31
Fruit, 31
Fuel:
  higher taxes on, 113

179